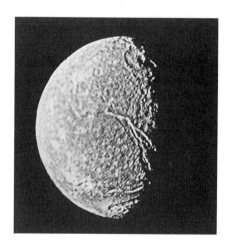

SMALL WORLDS

Exploring the 60 Moons of Our
Solar System

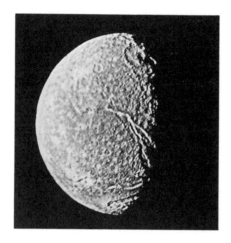

Joseph W. Kelch

Julian Messner

To the staff of the American Museum–Hayden Planetarium from July, 1981, to September, 1983—in particular, Clarence Brown, Allen Seltzer, Thomas Lesser, Dr. Kenneth Franklin, Joe Maddi, Joe Doti, Kai Eng, and Sandra Kitt, for giving me my start; to Karen, who shares my present and future; and to my parents, Jack and Mary Ann Kelch, whose dedication to love and family has provided the motivation for the achievement of all my dreams.

Photo sources:

Jet Propulsion Laboratory, Figs. 6-1, 6-2, 6-3, 6-4, 6-7, 6-8, 6-10; U.S. Naval Observatory, Fig. 8-1; AP/Wide World Photos, Figs. 9-1, 9-2, 9-3, 9-4; National Aeronautics and Space Administration, all other photos.

JULIAN MESSNER and colophon are trademarks of Simon & Schuster, Inc. Design by R STUDIO T. Manufactured in the United States of America.

Lib ed. 10 9 8 7 6 5 4 3 2 1
Hardcover ed. 10 9 8 7 6 5 4 3 2 1

Library of Congress Cataloging-in-Publication Data

Kelch, Joseph W., 1958-

Small worlds: exploring the 60 moons of our solar system / Joseph W. Kelch.

p.   cm.

Summary: Discusses the characteristics of each of the moons circling the planets of the solar system and manned space exploration.

space—Exploration—Juvenile literature. [1. Satellites. 2. Outer space—Exploration

QB401

523   8-6210

ISBN 0-671-70013-8   ISBN 0-671-70014-6 (Hardcover)

90-5452
CIP
AC

CONTENTS

1

TRAINING FOR A TRIP TO THE MOON 11
Looking at the Moon. 12
The First Sightings of Other Moons 13
Moons, Asteroids, and Comets 14
Getting the Measure of Things 15
The Motion of Moons 17
    Revolution 17
    Rotation 20
Reflectivity of Moons 20
Phases of the Moon. 21
Understanding Eclipses 22
    Solar Eclipses 22
    Lunar Eclipses 23
    Eclipses on Other Moons 23

2

THE EARTH'S MOON 24
Science Discovers the Moon 25
How Did Our Moon Form? 25

The Moon and the Oceans Play Tug-of-War 26
Our First Steps on the Moon 27
Two Moons in One 30
Coming Attractions: Back to the Moon 32
Launching Objects from the Moon 32
Factories on the Moon 32
Living on the Moon 37

3

MARS: RULER OF MINIMOONS 38
Mysterious Missing Moons 39
Fear and Terror, or Phobos and Deimos 40
Small Moons or Space Stations? 41
Black Moons with Strange Shapes 42
Will Phobos Collide with Mars? 48
The Countdown to Phobos Has Begun 48

4

JUPITER: FORBIDDEN SMALL WORLDS 51
The Galileans: Callisto, Ganymede, Europa,
and Io 52
Robots and Moon Mines 52
*A Great Discovery and Centuries
of Mystery* 53
*Callisto: The Crater Capital of the
Solar System* 53
Ganymede: The Planet-Sized Moon 56
Europa: Ice-Fishing, Anyone? 58
Io: The Most Violent of Moons 59
The Other Moons of Jupiter: Swarms
of Rocks 64
*Amalthea and Himalia: Largest of
the Small* 64

Thebe (and Friends): Asteroid Moons 64
Metis and Andrastea: Guardians of
  the Ring 65
Ananke, Carme, Pasiphae, and Sinope:
  The Far Outposts 65
Leda, Lysithea, and Elara: A Polar View
  of Jupiter 65

5

SATURN: RINGS AND MOONS 67
Saturn's Seventeen Moons—or Maybe
  Twenty-Three? 67
Titan: The Best Moon of Them All 68
  What? Smog on a Moon? 68
  Resources on Titan 70
Hyperion, Iapetus, and Phoebe: The Suburbs
  of Saturn 71
  Hyperion: The Tumbling Moon 71
  Iapetus: Two Moons in One 72
  Phoebe: A Dusty Wayward Intruder 74
On the Way in toward the Rings 75
  Rhea: Another Two-Faced Moon 75
  Dione: A Moon with a Moon 77
  Tethys: A Moon with Two Moons 78
  Enceladus: A Moon like a Mirror 78
  Mimas: Bashed and Broken 80
  Janus and Epimetheus: The Dancing
    Moons 80
The Rings: Stones, Snowballs, and Braided
  Bands 81
The Innermost Moons of Saturn 82
  Pandora and Prometheus: The Shepherd
    Moons 83
  Atlas (and Company): Midget Moons 83

6 URANUS: HOME OF SURPRISING MOONS 84

A New Challenge for *Voyager* 85

The Solar System Grows by One Planet and Five
Moons 86

The Five Major Moons of Uranus 87

*Oberon: Craters Splashed with Muddy
Water* 87

Titania: Giant Cracks 87

*Umbriel: Dark Craters and a Mysterious
Bright Ring* 89

Ariel: A Canyon World 90

Miranda: The Strangest of All Moons 90

The Newest Members of the Uranian
System 94

7 NEPTUNE: HIJACKER OF MOONS 97

Neptune: Storms, Blue Skies, and Moons 99

*The Inner Moons: More Ring
Shepherds?* 100

Nereid: Small and Bright 103

Triton: A Most Interesting World 104

The Approach to Triton 104

Ice Volcanoes and Geysers 104

Triton's Beginnings 106

8 PLUTO: THE ROAD NEVER TRAVELED 109

The Oddities of Pluto 109

Charon: Ferryman of the Underworld 110

The Origins of Pluto and Charon 112

Eclipses That Reveal All 112

An Imaginary Visit to Charon 114

9 JUST A FEW BILLION MORE SMALL WORLDS 115

Asteroids 116

Celestial Missing Links 116

Unusual Worlds with Unusual
Beginnings 117

Asteroids with Moons 118

Meteorites: Clues to the Asteroids 118

The Mother Lode of Space 119

Comets 120

The Most Abundant of Small Worlds 120

What to Do with a Comet 123

A CHECKLIST OF MOONS 127

INDEX 149

1
TRAINING FOR
A TRIP TO
THE MOON

You may be dreaming about making a trip to the moon someday. It certainly is a possibility worth thinking about. After all, only a few years have passed since people laughed at the few dreamers and inventors who believed that humans would one day fly in airplanes.

But if you are someday asked to go on an expedition to explore the moon, you might well ask: which moon?

You would need to ask because we are no longer aware of only one moon in our Solar System. We know there are at least sixty! Few people realize that the sky is full of moons, and that these moons are strange and exciting small worlds just waiting to be explored. These moons have always been there, of course, but we did not know about them. Recent space exploration has brought many surprises, especially concerning these small worlds.

Moons come in many sizes, shapes, and colors. Some are shaped like peanuts or potatoes. They come in colors such as orange, red, black, and white. Some are covered with ice and some with steaming volcanoes. In the future, we may find many uses for these small worlds as space stations, space factories, or even as places to make our home. This book will tell you about the many exciting moons that we have discovered so far.

Before you can travel to our many moons and find out more about them, however, you will need to prepare for the trip. You will need to look into the past as well as the future. But first you will need to understand a few facts about outer space.

LOOKING AT THE MOON

The Solar System is usually thought of as the sun and a family of nine planets moving in a regular fashion. But ours is a very active Solar System, full of speeding worlds colliding, exploding, and being born. Sometimes we even have visitors that seem to come from far off in the universe. For example, we were graced by the appearance of Halley's comet during the winter and spring of 1985-86. It is just one of probably billions of such bodies that circle the sun, most at such tremendous distances that they can never be seen from the earth. Meteors flash across our sky every night, remains of rocks called meteoroids that burn up as they enter our atmosphere.

Of course, there is also the Moon. Most people think of a moonlit night as romantic. The light is soft, barely revealing the details of the landscape. Another world is seen floating in the sky. It is a place of mystery and fascination. But it is also a place from which there could someday come great stories of courage and passion so far unknown to the inhabitants of Earth. After we think for just a few moments along these lines, the Moon becomes for us a spellbinding part of the sky.

Yet many people today tend to ignore the Moon. This was probably not the case in centuries past. Indeed, the most ancient of human creatures must have gazed in wonder at the Moon. They must have puzzled at the way it would appear at times in the night sky, slowly changing its shape, shrinking, and even disappearing. Sometimes they would catch a glimpse of it in the daytime sky as well. They saw a great power in the Moon and began to worship it as a god. In fact, the whole sky was thought to be filled with gods. The ancient peoples told stories, known today as myths, about the many different powers that ruled the universe. The planets were named after some of these mythical characters. Some groups of stars we call constellations were named after human heroes who also appeared in the stories.

Most people believed that the objects in the sky circled the earth. It was logical to believe this, since the earth was not obviously moving. Besides, the earth was the home of all life, and therefore the center of the universe. The gods, in the form of heavenly bodies, circled above to observe and guide the actions of human beings.

Even when the lights in the sky ceased to be thought of as gods, and Judaism and Christianity arose to replace many of the earlier pagan religions, it was assumed that the Judeo-Christian God had placed Earth at the center of His creation.

THE FIRST SIGHTINGS OF OTHER MOONS

In 1610, a man named Galileo Galilei began to study the sky, using his new telescope. While gazing at the planet Jupiter, he noticed some tiny points of light. He was able to see these dots night after night, but he became aware that they were in different places about the planet each night. He realized that they were circling Jupiter. This was the first time anyone had suspected the existence of moons about other worlds.

Galileo got into a great deal of trouble because of what he saw. Some people did not want to believe in his discovery, since it seemed to suggest that our planet was not the center of everything, that other worlds might circle distant planets rather than Earth.

Gradually, with continued discovery, people began to realize how large the universe was and that the earth was far from being the center of everything. Many more moons were discovered, not only around Jupiter, but also around many other planets of our Solar System. By the end of the nineteenth century, twenty-two moons, including our own, were known. Mars was known to have at least two, Jupiter five, Saturn nine, Uranus four, and Neptune one. Including the eight known planets of the time, this meant thirty worlds were known to exist, not counting the asteroids. This was five times the number known to the ancient civilizations of the world. Without telescopes, these earlier peoples had been aware only of our Moon and of the five planets that could be seen with their unaided eyes.

During the twentieth century, the Solar-System population explosion continued. The discovery of many small moons brought to twelve the total believed to be circling Jupiter. Another moon was glimpsed circling Saturn. One apiece were also added for Uranus and Neptune. By the time the *Voyager* spacecraft lifted from the launchpad of Cape Canaveral in 1977, forty-one members of the Solar System had been identified as planets or moons. Thousands of asteroids had also been observed, though few of these were of very great size.

MOONS, ASTEROIDS, AND COMETS

Recent spacecraft explorations have made us aware of additional moons. The exact number is not known with certainty, since some of these moons were only glimpsed and their orbits have not been determined. The total seems to be at least sixty, with as many as twenty-three of these orbiting Saturn. (See the drawing of the Solar System and its moons in the middle of the color insert at the center of this book.) Only Mercury and Venus appear to be without any companions. More than 3,300 asteroids have also been catalogued. These range from one kilometer up to one thousand kilometers in diameter. We have also taken close-up pictures of Halley's comet that have helped us to find out just what such spectacular cometary visitors are like.

In this book, we shall focus our attention mostly on the moons. Most of the ''larger'' small worlds of the Solar System are found among this group. We shall finish up with a look at the special small worlds known as asteroids and comets, since they may be of great importance to us in the future. The idea of this book is not to provide a great many facts and figures. Instead, it will give us an opportunity to go exploring and see what kinds of wonders we shall find.

Before setting out, however, let us get some supplies together. By *supplies* we mean a basic store of information on what moons are and how they work. This way we shall be more prepared for what we find.

I should mention that the word *Moon* will be capitalized when it refers to Earth's "natural satellite." This will help keep us from getting it confused with all the other moons.

GETTING THE MEASURE OF THINGS

First, let us discuss the way we shall be measuring things. Most of the world today uses the metric system. The metric system includes units such as meters, kilometers, liters, and degrees Celsius. The system used in the United States is called the English system. It uses units such as inches, miles, gallons, and degrees Fahrenheit. The problem with the English units is that they do not break down easily into smaller units. For example, a fraction of a mile is not easily converted into inches. If someone asks you to tell how many inches are in 0.647 mile, you will have to do some pretty complex math to get an answer. The English system is thus not very effective when you want to understand and deal with fractions of a unit.

In the metric system, meters are broken down into smaller units that are simply one tenth of the preceding unit. One tenth of a meter is a decimeter. One tenth of a decimeter is a centimeter. One tenth of a centimeter is a millimeter, and so on. These units then correspond to the values following the decimal point in a number. For example, 0.647 meter is simply 6 decimeters plus 4 centimeters plus 7 millimeters. You could also say it is 6.47 decimeters or 64.7 centimeters or 647 millimeters. Whenever we multiply or divide by ten, we simply have to move the decimal point one place to the right or left. Notice that all the units have *meter* as part of the word. The part before *meter,* the prefix, indicates what part of a meter we mean. *Deci-* means one tenth, *centi-* means one hundredth, and *milli-* means one thousandth. We shall generally use a unit bigger than the meter: the kilometer. *Kilo-* means one thousand, so a kilometer is one thousand meters. To satisfy any curiosity you may have about the size of a kilometer, we shall tell you that one kilometer is equal to about 0.621 mile. (See the distance-conversion table on pg. 16.)

Celsius degrees are better than Fahrenheit degrees when temperature

> ## Conversion Table for Metric and English Distance Units
>
> ### Metric
> 10 millimeters (mm) = 1 centimeter (cm)
> 100 mm = 10 cm = 1 decimeter (dm)
> 1000 mm = 100 cm = 10 dm = 1 meter (m)
> 1000 m = 1 kilometer (km) = 0.621 mile (mi)
>
> ### English
> 12 inches (in.) = 1 foot (ft)
> 36 in. = 3 ft = 1 yard (yd)
> 63,360 in. = 5280 ft = 1760 yd = 1 mile (mi)
>
> 149,500,000 km = 1 astronomical unit (AU) = 92,900,000 mi

is measured. This is because two of the most important temperatures have round, even-number values in degrees Celsius. The freezing point of water is 32 degrees Fahrenheit—an inconvenient number to deal with. The freezing point in degrees Celsius is simply 0 degrees Celsius. The boiling point of water, which is 212 degrees on the Fahrenheit scale, is 100 degrees Celsius. There is another temperature scale used in science. It is called the Kelvin scale, and is expressed in units called kelvins. It is easy to convert degrees Celsius to kelvins: just add 273 to the Celsius temperature. Zero kelvin is absolute zero, the lowest possible temperature. At absolute zero, it is so cold that even molecules and atoms are unable to move. Absolute zero is −273 degrees Celsius, or about −459 degrees Fahrenheit. The coldest naturally occurring temperature ever recorded on Earth was about −125 degrees Fahrenheit, which is about −87 degrees Celsius or 176 kelvins. We shall use mostly the Celsius scale in this book.

Almost all scientists use only metric units, and, since this book deals with science, we shall use mostly metric units, too. A nonmetric unit is often used in astronomy, however, especially when our Solar System is discussed. It is called an astronomical unit, or AU. One astronomical unit is equal to the distance between the sun and Earth, or about 149.5 million kilometers. Usually, the distances we mention in this book will be given in kilometers, but you might like to convert some of them into astronomical units. In any case, try to remember the distance between the earth and the sun in kilometers. Doing so will help you get a sense of the size of the other measurements given in this book.

THE MOTION OF MOONS

Moons, or natural satellites, as they are sometimes called, are objects in our Solar System that travel around a body other than the sun. Moons thus include any objects traveling around planets, and the few smaller bodies that travel around some of the asteroids. The special machines that we launch into paths around the earth are almost always simply called satellites, so that they will not be confused with these natural satellites. There are two major types of motion that are typical of moons, or natural satellites. You will need to learn about these motions before you begin your journey.

Revolution

The path an object, such as a moon, follows through space when it travels around another object is called an orbit. The orbiting motion of such an object is called *revolution,* and the orbiting object is said to revolve.

Objects are able to revolve, or follow orbits, because of gravity, the force that keeps you and me from drifting away from the surface of the earth. All matter in the universe has gravity. The more matter you place into a given amount of space, the greater is the gravity that results. The body weight you measure here on the earth is caused by gravity. The mass of your body could also be measured. Mass is a measurement of the amount of matter that makes up an object. The mass of an object does not change if you take the object away from a source of gravity. Weight does because it relies on gravity. When you determine the weight of something, you are actually finding out how hard gravity is pulling on it. In space, far from any source of gravity, you would be weightless. You would still have mass, however—otherwise, you would not exist.

If you go outside and throw a ball very gently straight ahead, you will see that the ball moves forward a little, but also falls toward the ground. If you throw the ball harder, it moves farther forward before hitting the ground. Imagine that there were no limit to how hard you could throw the ball. It would travel farther and farther before reaching the ground. Remember, though, that the earth is a sphere. That means that as the ball travels forward, the ground is also curving downward away from the ball. If the ball traveled forward fast enough, the ground would fall away from the ball at the same rate the ball fell toward the ground. The ball would get no closer to the ground and would continue to travel around the earth, unless something slowed down the rate at which the ball traveled forward. The ball would have achieved orbit. (See Figure 1-1.)

Unfortunately, here, near the surface of the earth, it would be impossible for the ball to orbit the planet successfully. The atmosphere of our planet would not allow the ball to remain at the necessary velocity. Friction at orbital speeds would heat the ball so much that it would burn up almost

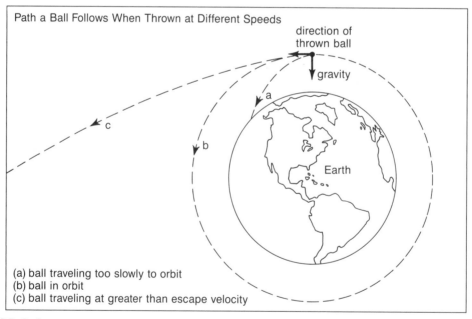

Path a Ball Follows When Thrown at Different Speeds

direction of thrown ball

gravity

a

c

b

Earth

(a) ball traveling too slowly to orbit
(b) ball in orbit
(c) ball traveling at greater than escape velocity

FIGURE 1-1

instantly, as do the meteors we see flashing across the night sky. However, if you took the ball into space, above the atmosphere, it could remain in orbit, traveling around and around the earth. The speed you would need to reach orbit just above the atmosphere is about 25,000 kilometers per hour.

If you threw the ball at or a little faster than this speed of 25,000 kilometers per hour, the ground would at first fall away from the ball more quickly than the ball moved downward due to gravity. The ball would in effect begin to rise higher relative to the earth's surface. As it did, gravity would slow it down, and it would then begin falling toward the ground. However, as it fell, it would gain speed and once again begin to rise. This motion toward and away from the ground would form an oval, or elliptical, orbit. All objects in our Solar System travel in orbits that are at least somewhat elliptical, rather than perfectly circular. In many cases, however, the difference between closest and farthest approach to the parent body is very minor. Earth, for example, orbits the sun at an average distance of 149.5 million kilometers. It is as much as 151.2 million and as little as 146.4 million kilometers away from the sun during the course of each orbit. The degree to which an orbit is elliptical can be expressed by a value called *eccentricity.* An orbit that has an eccentricity of 0 is circular. One whose eccentricity is only slightly less than 1 is highly elliptical. The eccentricity of Earth's orbit is 0.017.

Eccentricities of 1 or greater indicate paths in which the moving object will not travel in a repeating orbit—in other words, an object in such a path will escape from the system. Consider the example of the ball once again. If you threw the ball fast enough, its path would have an eccentricity greater than 1. The ball would continue to travel away from the earth's surface. It would not slow down enough to fall back toward the surface and would escape into space. The velocity necessary to achieve this is called escape velocity. The escape velocity from Earth is a little over 40,000 kilometers per hour. The Apollo astronauts traveling to the Moon needed to reach this velocity in order to escape from Earth's gravity.

Since moons travel in orbits, they are moving around their parent body at the velocity necessary in order for them to remain near it without colliding with it. Maintaining an orbit can be tricky, because the gravity of the sun is also affecting the moons. The orbits of most known moons turn out to be quite stable, however. You certainly do not have to worry about Earth's Moon falling onto your hometown anytime soon. The orbits of most moons as they revolve are nearly circular, very much like the orbits of the planets. Their distances from the planets do not change very much. They usually orbit close to or directly above the equator of the parent planet. However, as you will see, there are exceptions to all these general rules.

Rotation

The motion of moons is not limited to revolution. Moons also spin about on their axes (lines passing through their poles), in a motion called *rotation*. Most moons have been found to rotate in such a way that they always keep the same face toward the planet they circle. This is true of our Moon as well. Most moons thus rotate once every time they orbit their parent planet. A "day" on a moon is generally the same length of time as one orbit.

REFLECTIVITY OF MOONS

Many of the moons discovered in our Solar System were found through the use of telescopes. We can see them because of the light they reflect back to us from space. Not all moons reflect the same amount of light, however. The amount reflected depends on the material that makes up the surface. Moons with icy surfaces reflect much more light than do moons covered with dark rock. Earth reflects about 39 percent of the light it receives from the sun. Our Moon reflects about 11 percent. These reflectivity values are often expressed in terms of a quantity called *albedo* (al-bée-doe). Earth's albedo is 0.39, since it reflects 39/100 of the light that strikes it. The darkest objects in the Solar System have albedos of about 0.04. The brightest objects have albedos of nearly 1. The brightest moon, Enceladus, which orbits Saturn, has such an albedo, indicating that it reflects almost all of the light reaching it from the sun. If our Moon had an albedo that great, it would seem to shine almost as brightly as a second sun.

The side of any moon (except our own) that is facing Earth is always the side lit up by the Sun. That is because all of the moons in the Solar System except ours are more distant from the sun than Earth is. When we look toward them, the sun is effectively either at our backs or between us and the moon we are observing.

PHASES OF THE MOON

As the Moon orbits Earth, it is seen in different parts of the sky. We see it sometimes in the night sky and sometimes during the daylight hours. As you have certainly noticed, the Moon also looks different at various times. It seems to change shape, passing through what are called *phases*.

The cycle of phases begins with what is called the new Moon. The new-Moon phase occurs when the Moon is between Earth and the sun. Light from the sun then shines on the side of the Moon that is facing away from Earth. The side toward us is dark. Therefore, you cannot see the new Moon. The new Moon rises and sets at just about the same time as the sun.

As a few days go by, the Moon begins to move out of line with the sun. It sets about an hour later each night, remaining above the horizon after the sun sets. You can then begin to see the Moon in the western sky shortly after sunset. Just a small sliver of the Moon is lit up at first, the lit edge pointing toward the setting sun. Each night the lit portion grows larger. A moon in this phase is known as a waxing crescent Moon.

About a week after the new Moon, you can see the Moon in the form of a half circle. Many people call this phase a half-Moon. Remember, though, that a half of the Moon is also facing away from Earth, and half of the part facing toward Earth is unlit. You are really seeing only half of half of the Moon, or one quarter of it. So the Moon in this phase is called the first-quarter Moon. It rises in the east at noon and sets at midnight. It is in the south at sunset.

During the next week, the Moon appears in the eastern sky at sunset. Its lit portion is getting larger than it was during the quarter phase. The Moon in this phase is called the waxing gibbous Moon.

Two weeks after the new Moon, we reach what is probably the most familiar of the Moon's phases. The Moon then rises in the east just as the sun is setting in the west, and sets in the west just as the sun is rising in the east. It appears as a full circle of light in a clear night sky. The Moon in this phase is, of course, called the full Moon. On clear nights, a full Moon can be bright enough to cast shadows.

As the next week progresses, the Moon's lit portion begins to become smaller. The Moon again begins to approach the sun's position in the sky, though it is still visible mostly at night. It is in the waning gibbous phase. It does not rise until after sunset.

One week after full Moon, the Moon again appears as a half circle. The Moon in this phase is called the third- or last-quarter Moon. It now rises at around midnight and is in the south at sunrise. The lit side of the circle points toward the sun.

As the following week closes out, the Moon again becomes a small crescent. It is found in the eastern sky at sunrise and has already set by the time the sun sets in the evening. Finally, about four weeks after the cycle began, we are back to the new Moon, which disappears from the sky once again for a couple of days before returning to start another journey around the earth.

UNDERSTANDING ECLIPSES

The passage of one heavenly body between two others can prevent the light from the outer bodies from reaching one another. This blockage of light is called an *eclipse.* As you will learn, eclipses can be of several different types.

Solar Eclipses

Usually the new Moon passes just slightly above or below the sun, rather than directly in front of it. Occasionally, though, it does pass directly in front, and its shadow then falls upon the earth. Such an event is called an eclipse of the sun, or *solar eclipse,* and is quite rare. It is especially rare if the sun and Moon are lined up just right, so that the Moon completely covers the sun. Such an eclipse is called a total solar eclipse. Most people see only a partial eclipse even when a total eclipse is visible elsewhere. This is because an eclipse's path of totality on Earth is very narrow, usually less than one hundred kilometers wide. These total eclipses are also very short, because the Moon barely covers the sun in the sky and moves across it quickly. The maximum length of a total solar eclipse is a little over seven minutes. At any single location on the earth, a total solar eclipse is seen only once on an average of over three hundred years. To see one yourself, you will therefore probably have to do some traveling.

Lunar Eclipses

There is also a type of eclipse that can occur at full Moon. Such an eclipse is called a *lunar eclipse.* It happens when the Moon passes into the shadow of the earth. Lunar eclipses are more common than total solar eclipses, and there is a good chance you will be able to see one, if you have not already. Such eclipses can last nearly two hours and are visible over an entire hemisphere (half) of the earth. The Moon usually appears a dark rusty red or brown during a total lunar eclipse, because the only light from the sun that reaches it is first refracted, or bent, into the shadow of the earth by our atmosphere. From the Moon, a total lunar eclipse would appear as a solar eclipse does from the earth, with the sun blocked out—in this case, by the earth. From the Moon, Earth would seem to be ringed by a bright red glow of sunlight bending through the air—no doubt a beautiful sight.

Eclipses on Other Moons

Many of the other moons of the Solar System go through phases, and many are involved in eclipses as well. To see them, it will be necessary to journey out to these worlds. An eclipse of the sun by the planet Jupiter, as seen from one of its outer moons, might be quite spectacular. From the surface of Rhea, a moon of Saturn, you could probably see many other moons in various phases scattered all over the sky at the same time as the eclipse was visible.

All this information on moons, measurement, phases, and eclipses should help you on your journey. I hope you will find the trip interesting. Perhaps as a result of it, you will make such a trip for real someday. For now, slip on your imaginary spacesuit and let's get moving!

THE EARTH'S MOON

Even before the first civilizations, the motions and appearances of the Moon were already familiar to our ancestors and were already being put to practical use. For example, the cycles of the Moon's phases served as one of the first clocks. The time it required to complete a full cycle divided the year up into month-long pieces that signaled the approaching changes of season.

The Moon was also an object of superstition for our ancestors. For example, there was an ancient belief that if the light of the full Moon fell onto a sleeping person, insanity would result. Our word *lunacy,* from *luna,* the Latin word for *moon,* stems from this belief. Religion also had links to the Moon, which used to be considered a god or goddess in many old religions. Even today, the Moon helps decide when some religious holidays, such as Easter and Passover, will take place. For example, Easter must always fall on the first Sunday after the first full Moon after the first day of spring.

SCIENCE DISCOVERS THE MOON

It may seem hard to believe that just four hundred years ago, people knew nothing about the surface of the Moon. However, a look at it with the unaided eye really does reveal very little. If the Moon is in the sky now as you are reading this, go out and see for yourself.

When Galileo Galilei took a very primitive new invention called the telescope and turned it toward the Moon, many fascinating details were suddenly visible. Galileo's observations showed for the first time just how violent the Solar System must have been in the past. Strange features, such as the craters of the Moon, indicated that great forces had been at work.

For hundreds of years, astronomers argued about whether the lunar craters were formed by volcanic eruptions or meteoroid impacts. Craters formed in both ways are found here on Earth. Probably the most famous crater formed by meteoroid impact is Barringer Meteor Crater, in Arizona. It looks very much like a smaller version of the large lunar craters visible through ordinary telescopes. Scientists are now quite certain that the lunar craters were formed in much the same way—that is, through meteoroid impact rather than volcanic eruptions.

When the larger bodies of the Solar System were formed, about five billion years ago, many pieces of rock were left over. These collided with the young planets and their satellites. We see the record of these collisions on the surface of many of the worlds that have been studied. The Moon's surface serves as one of the best examples of the effects of these events. The Moon had no atmosphere or water to erode its surface, so the craters formed by the meteoroid impacts have remained very much as they appeared the day they were created, despite the fact that many of them are several billion years old.

(You may wish to consult "A Checklist of Moons," which begins on p. 127 of this book. The checklist contains a great deal of information on Earth's Moon, as well as on the other moons of the Solar System.)

HOW DID OUR MOON FORM?

Many attempts have been made over the years to explain the origin and development of the Moon. It is now thought that the Solar System in its early days was full of dust and gas. This material began to gather together in lumps. Gravity then pulled more dust and rocks toward the lumps, which began to grow. In this way, both large and small bodies were formed. The large bodies became planets. Some of the smaller bodies were attracted by the gravity of the young planets. Some of these smaller bodies crashed to the surface of the planets. However, others fell into orbit around the planets instead. These bodies became the moons. Our Moon probably formed in this manner.

When matter piled up together in this way to form planets and moons, great pressure developed near the center of each body, and this pressure produced heat. Heat was also produced by radioactive minerals, which were present in large quantities at the time the Solar System was formed. Meteoroid impacts added more heat. All this heat caused the rocky cores of the early planets and moons to become molten, or liquid. The core of the earth is still molten today, as seen in the eruptions of volcanoes.

There is evidence that the Moon also had a molten core a long time ago. The so-called lunar seas are ancient lava flows, many of which were probably triggered by large meteoroid impacts. Since the Moon is rather small compared to Earth, its core cooled much more quickly than that of Earth. Today, it is likely that the Moon's core is solid.

A world with a solid core is said to be "geologically dead." This means that very little can happen to change the interior or the surface of the world without interference from outside. There is very little chance of Moonquakes occurring, for example, since quakes generally occur when a thin solid crust slides over a molten interior. The fact that the Moon has long been geologically dead, together with the fact that there is no water or atmosphere to cause erosion, explains why lunar craters have lasted so long. In the absence of a major meteoroid impact—or of large-scale human activity on the Moon—the familiar face of Earth's natural satellite is unlikely to change very much for a long time to come.

THE MOON AND THE OCEANS PLAY TUG-OF-WAR

The Moon has effects on the surface of the earth and helps to cause change here on our world. Tides are caused by the gravitational pull of the Moon on the earth. The extent of tides depends on the alignment of the sun and the Moon. When these two bodies are either in the same direction from Earth or on opposite sides of it, the greatest tides are produced. This means that such tides are produced when the Moon is new or full. These large tides are called *spring tides.* When the Moon and the sun are at 90 degrees from each other in the sky, which occurs at first and last quarter, the tides are smallest, and are called *neap tides.* Over millions of years, the ebb and flow of tides erode and change the shape of our seashores. The pull of the Moon also slightly affects the crust of the earth and may be a factor in triggering earthquakes.

OUR FIRST STEPS ON THE MOON

The Moon is the only world, other than the earth, on which people have ever stood. Between 1969 and 1972, there were six successful Apollo missions to the surface of our nearest neighbor in space. Each visit lasted only a few days, and so the surface of this ancient world was changed only by the addition of some footprints and tire tracks. (See Color Photo 1 in the insert at the center of this book.) The astronauts also left behind a few scientific instruments that could be controlled from the earth, allowing us to continue observations after the astronauts had left for home. (See Figure 2-1.) Hundreds of kilograms of Moon rock were returned for examination. This helped us form a clearer picture of the history of the Moon's surface. (See Figures 2-2 and 2-3.)

Although impacts by large meteoroids are now rare in our Solar System, impacts by smaller ones happen all the time. Our atmosphere protects us from the impact of all but the largest of such rocks, but many smaller ones enter our atmosphere, as is obvious if you watch the sky at night and see the large number of meteors that streak across.

Many meteors do continue to bombard the Moon. Most of these are so small that their effect is invisible to the unaided eye. Scientists studying the rocks returned by the Apollo astronauts discovered microscopic craters in some of the samples. These craters were caused by a rain of tiny particles from space that broke up the surface material. Such bombard-

FIGURE 2-1 *During the six successful missions to the surface of the Moon, astronauts explored dozens of miles of lunar terrain. Many of the scientific instruments that were used continued to function long after the explorers returned to Earth.*

FIGURE 2-2 *Astronaut Charles M. Duke, Jr., of* Apollo 16 *collects lunar samples near Plum Crater on the Moon.*

FIGURE 2-3 *This is one of the Moon rocks returned by the Apollo missions. Because of the close-up view, the rock may seem large. Actually, it is only about 14 centimeters (5.5 inches) in length. This is a basaltic rock, the same kind of rock found on the ocean floors of the earth.*

ment helped bring about a very slow erosion that has produced a lunar "soil" called *regolith.* This soil also contains glassy pieces formed by the melting of rocks when larger meteoroids crashed into the Moon. The crash of each large meteoroid probably threw this glassy material over an area of hundreds of square kilometers. Pieces of smashed rock that are also found in the regolith are additional indications of this impact process.

TWO MOONS IN ONE

There are really two different kinds of lunar surface: heavily cratered highlands and smoother lunar "seas," or *maria. (Maria* is not pronounced like the woman's name. The accent is on *mar.)* There are very few large

FIGURE 2-4 *The earth seen near the edge of the Moon, from the window of the* Apollo 14 *lunar module shortly before beginning the descent to the surface. The very alien cratered surface of our natural satellite is plainly visible.*

craters in the maria, which seems to have been formed for the most part after the period of large meteoroid impacts. The rocks in the maria are mostly of a kind called basalt. Basalt is commonly formed in volcanic processes. (It is also the main component of the earth's ocean floor.) Scientists have dated these lunar basalt rocks as being between 2.5 billion and 4 billion years old. Volcanic processes apparently occurred on the Moon that long ago.

The cratered highland regions of the Moon (see Figure 2-4) are composed of an assortment of different rocks that date back as much as 4.6 billion years. They were formed at just about the time the Moon finally cooled enough to form a solid surface, or crust. These rocks are among the oldest in the Solar System.

COMING ATTRACTIONS: BACK TO THE MOON

The late 1980s were expected to be a busy time for the United States in exploring space. The *Challenger* space-shuttle disaster has slowed progress somewhat, however. For example, there is still no definite plan to return to the Moon any time soon, despite the fact that many years have now passed since the Apollo Moon Project. However, we can still look forward to a fairly busy future in space.

Launching Objects from the Moon

A recent report by the National Commission on Space has presented us with a plan for making good use of our talents and the resources of outer space. The Moon plays a major role in this plan. Launching rockets into space from the surface of our planet is a difficult and expensive task, but the Moon may help us to find an easier way. The key to the problem is gravity. We on Earth are always under the influence of 1 *g,* a *g* being a measure of the gravitational strength at the surface of the earth. The gravitational strength at the surface of the Moon is much less than 1 *g,* and so objects would weigh less on the Moon than they do on Earth. For example, spacecraft are much lighter on the Moon (see Figure 2-5). Space stations would also be lighter. The first space station planned for the 1990s would weigh one hundred fifty tons on the earth, but only one sixth that, or about twenty-five tons, on the Moon. Such an object would be much lighter and easier to move on the Moon than on the earth. Although it will not be feasible to launch our first space station from the Moon, in the future many other large space structures could be built there and launched from there. Such launching would save a great deal of energy.

Factories on the Moon

If we had to depend on getting materials from the earth in order to build something on the Moon, we would, in effect, be launching the material twice—once from Earth and then once from the Moon. That would hardly represent a saving of time, money, or energy. No, there must be a better solution.

Fortunately, studies of the Moon rocks returned by Apollo missions

FIGURE 2-5 *This sequence of three images (see following pages) shows the liftoff of Apollo 15's lunar module from the surface of the Moon. The pictures were transmitted from a camera mounted on the lunar roving vehicle, which the astronauts had used during their stay. This tiny spacecraft was able to transport two humans safely from the surface of the Moon into orbit, where the command module was waiting to take them back to Earth. This same spacecraft could never achieve orbit from the surface of the earth, whose gravitation is much greater than that of the Moon.*

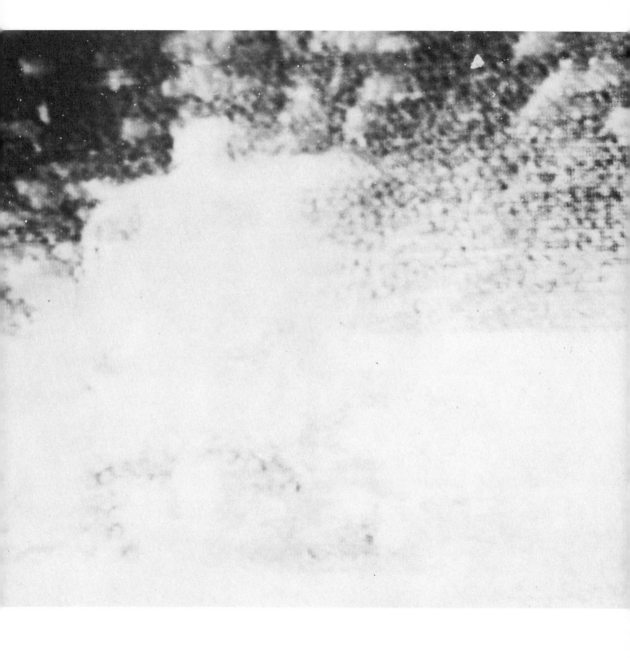

FIGURE 2-6 *Because of its weak gravity and its wealth of valuable resources, the Moon will one day be dotted with mining colonies providing needed materials for the whole Solar System.*

indicate that there are many useful industrial resources available right on the Moon. Many materials for building on the Moon would not need to be sent from the earth. For instance, the Moon contains many aluminum and titanium ores that would be very useful in construction. Nickel, magnesium, and uranium ores there would also be of use, as would oxygen, one of the most abundant elements in lunar soil. (See Figure 2-6.)

The National Commission report described a program in which a permanent station would be set up on the lunar surface in the year 2005. By 2020, large-scale production of propellant would occur and manufacturing facilities would exist by that date.

The carrying out of scientific research would be an important reason for being on the Moon. For example, telescopes would function much better on the Moon, which has no atmosphere to obscure the view, than they do on Earth. Observatories on the far side of the Moon would be able to gather information on infrared and radio objects in deep space without interference from earthly sources.

Living on the Moon

Some people now imagine a day when the Moon will be home to thousands of humans living in comfort. Some of you may one day roll out of bed and look out the window across a rolling gray landscape dotted with craters. You may see a small launchpad nearby being used to launch workers to an orbiting spaceport. A lunar "bus" may fly by a few meters above the surface, on its way to an observatory on the far side of the Moon. And, in the dark sky overhead, you may see your former home, the earth—blue and white with splotches of green—a place you might visit for the holidays, but no longer the place that you would call home.

MARS:
RULER OF
MINIMOONS

"**T**his is Vulcan 1 *transmitting landing sequence to International Space Authority on space station* Alexandria. *Range to touchdown: two thousand five hundred meters, approaching at thirty meters per second.*"

(PAUSE)

"Attitude nominal, fuel nominal, range nineteen hundred meters, twenty-seven meters per second. Crew secured and on station. Contact sensor probe deployed."

(PAUSE)

"Range one thousand meters, twenty-five meters per second. Landing-station anchor arms extended and armed. About one minute to contact."

(PAUSE)

"Range three hundred meters, fifteen meters per second. Computer approach procedure engaged."

(PAUSE)

"Range fifty meters, five meters per second. Many rocks down there. Range forty meters, four meters per second. Drifting slightly. Range twenty-five meters, two meters per second. Kicking up and drifting of dust seem to have stopped. Contact probe light on. Range eight meters, one meter per second. Anchor arm contact! Anchors fired. All engines stopped. Vulcan 1 *reports safe arrival on Phobos. Stand by for ship status."*

Sometime during the next forty years, a message like this will be sent across tens of millions of kilometers to Earth. It will describe our next landing on a new world, a moon of another planet. That moon, Phobos, is very small and might not seem very important in itself. We shall go there, though, because it is orbiting very close to the first planet that men and women will likely make their new home—Mars. From its tiny moon Phobos, the first expedition for descent to the red surface of the planet Mars will be prepared.

MYSTERIOUS MISSING MOONS

The second-most-closely-studied planet of the Solar System is the red planet Mars (the most studied is, of course, Earth). As one of our closest neighbors in space, Mars has been explored through telescopes and by spacecraft more than any of the other planets. Yet, it was only quite recently that humans discovered that Mars had any moons at all. Not until the space age was anything learned about them.

For a long time, it was believed that Mars did not have any moons. As telescopes improved, natural satellites were discovered orbiting Jupiter, Saturn, Uranus, and Neptune, but none were seen at the much closer distance of Mars. Many people did keep looking for Martian moons, however. There was even some speculation about moons in stories written more than two hundred years ago. For example, in "The Voyage to Laputa," one of the adventures in *Gulliver's Travels* (1727), Jonathan Swift tells of a people who were aware of two moons in orbit about Mars. In 1750, the French writer Voltaire also assigns two moons to Mars, in his story *Micromegas*.

By the middle of the 1800s, people had noticed a curious pattern to the number of moons known to be orbiting the planets. Mercury and Venus had none; Earth had one; Jupiter had four; and Saturn had eight. It seemed logical to expect Mars (which lies between Earth and Jupiter) to have two moons. Astronomers continued to search for these moons.

During the summer of 1877, Asaph Hall, an astronomer at the U.S. Naval Observatory in Washington, searched for moons of Mars. He used the most powerful telescope of the time, a twenty-six-inch refractor. Hall spent night after night searching the sky near Mars. Eventually, he became discouraged and was ready to give up. His wife, Angeline, however, urged him to try just one more time. Hall agreed, and in the early morning hours of August eleventh, he noticed a faint dot near Mars. He was very excited about the possibility that he was seeing a moon. However, the next several nights were cloudy, so he could not observe the region of Mars again until August sixteenth. When the skies finally cleared, the dotlike object was back. The next night he saw another object even closer to the planet. He quickly announced to the world his discovery of the two moons of Mars.

FEAR AND TERROR, OR PHOBOS AND DEIMOS

Hall named the two moons after the mythological sons of Mars, the ancient god of war. The inner moon was named Phobos (Fear), and the outer one, the first to be seen by Hall, was named Deimos (Terror).

These two moons are so faint that study of them proved very difficult. They were much smaller and dimmer than the moons of Jupiter that had been seen by Galileo. A further problem in observing these worlds was their proximity, or closeness, to Mars. Light from the planet would wash out the very faint light coming from them. It was necessary to have very good viewing conditions and the best telescopes in order to see them.

Interest in the moons was lessened as a result of the great interest in Mars itself. Astronomers were fascinated by reports of Martian polar caps, green areas, and strange crisscrossing lines that were being called canals by many. The observation of the "canals" led to the idea that there was intelligent life on Mars. Most astronomers spent their time observing the planet and ignoring its two little moons.

Some observations of these moons did take place, however, and information slowly began to come in. Phobos was observed to be about 15 kilometers in diameter—so small that 10 million objects its size could fit inside our own moon! Phobos orbits less than 6,000 kilometers above the planet. In contrast, the earth and the Moon are separated by a distance more than 50 times greater. Seen from the surface of Mars, Phobos would look only about one third the size our Moon does when seen from Earth. Also, if you were on the surface of Mars, you would see Phobos rise and set three times a day. Even more strangely, Phobos would seem to move across the sky in the wrong direction—that is, from west to east instead of from east to west, like our Moon. In fact, you might see Phobos rising at the same time and place the sun was setting. The second moon of Mars, Deimos, was found to be only half the size of Phobos. Deimos orbits at a height of about 18,000 kilometers. It would appear to be nothing other than a bright star in the Martian sky. (See "A Checklist of Moons," which begins on p. 127, for more information on Phobos and Deimos, as well as the other moons of the Solar System.)

Small Moons or Space Stations?

The small size of the Martian moons did raise questions about the way in which the moons came into being. Surely their history would be different from that of the other moons in the Solar System. Some people thought the moons might be former asteroids, somehow separated from the main belt between Mars and Jupiter and captured by the gravitational attraction of the red planet. Some people even thought that the moons might be hollow. In fact, it was suggested they might be space stations built by Martians! If that were true and the Martians could travel through space, people reasoned that the Martians might soon arrive to invade the earth. It was about this time that H.G. Wells published *War of the Worlds,* a fictional account of an attack from Mars.

Little solid information could be obtained about Mars and its moons until the beginning of the space age. Since Mars was thought to be the most likely planet to have living things, it was the one to which space probes in search of life were most quickly sent. Both the United States and the Soviet Union launched many missions, but up to the late 1980s only the American effort has had any real success in gaining data on the planet.

In November, 1964, the *Mariner 4* space probe lifted off on a seven-month journey to Mars. The probe was primitive by today's standards, but it did succeed in sending back the first close-range pictures of another planet. They showed Mars to be a planet that looked like much of our Moon: covered with craters. It was nothing like the planet many people had expected to find. There were no canals and no living things. The atmosphere was also found to be very thin, since the craters showed hardly any erosion and contained very little life-supporting oxygen. Although no direct pictures or other information on Phobos and Deimos came from *Mariner 4,* people could now safely assume that the two small bodies were indeed moons and not hollow space stations, since there were no Martians to have built such stations!

Black Moons with Strange Shapes

Four years later, just days after the successful *Apollo 11* Moon landing, *Mariner 6* and *Mariner 7* flew past Mars, taking a total of more than two hundred pictures. For the most part, these pictures confirmed the findings of *Mariner 4.* One picture, from *Mariner 7,* was special, however. It included the image of the moon Phobos against the surface of Mars. The surface of the little moon was almost completely black, much darker than that of Mars. No individual features could be seen. Phobos was not spherical, but somewhat elongated. Some described it as being potato-shaped.

The next visitor to Mars was *Mariner 9.* On November 14, 1971, this probe became the first human-made object ever to be placed in orbit about another planet. A great planet-wide dust storm was taking place at the time, however, and only a few dark spots could be seen on the planet. Besides providing information on the storm, there was little that *Mariner 9* could reveal about Mars itself, so, soon after its arrival, the spacecraft was made to seek out and photograph the moons of Mars.

Prior to the explorations of *Mariner 9,* the orbits of Phobos and Deimos were not known very accurately. The spacecraft began by taking pictures of the moons at a great distance. These pictures were used to get a precise understanding of the moons' orbits. This knowledge allowed for much better close-up pictures later on, since scientists could predict exactly where the moons would be.

Mariner 9 also revealed Phobos to be a very rough, heavily cratered world. The craters were assumed to be caused by meteoroid impacts. Phobos appeared to be about 20 by 25 kilometers, confirming the elongated shape suggested by the *Mariner 7* picture. Deimos, with dimensions of about 10 by 16 kilometers, was not spherical either. Both Phobos and Deimos were found to keep the same face toward Mars at all times, just as our Moon does relative to Earth.

Both moons were indeed very dark—in fact, among the darkest objects ever observed in the Solar System. They reflected only about 7 percent of the sunlight that reached their surfaces. Their orbits were quite circular, and were fixed almost directly above the equator of the planet. This fact made it seem unlikely that they might have been captured asteroids. Such a captured asteroid would more likely travel in an elongated orbit not lined up with the planet's equator. It seemed that new theories on the origin of the Martian moons were needed.

The *Viking 1* and *Viking 2* orbiters reached Mars in the summer of 1976. Although most public attention was focused on the search for life on the red planet, the orbiters did much to extend our knowledge of the Martian neighborhood.

In 1977, in honor of the hundredth anniversary of Asaph Hall's discovery, Phobos and Deimos were studied closely by the *Viking* spacecraft. The information that had come from *Mariner 9* was checked and improved with more accurate data. Pictures of the two moons' shadows moving across the planet were used to help map the planet and find the exact position of the *Viking* landers. (See Figure 3-1.) Some of the best pictures ever taken by a flyby or orbiter spacecraft were those sent back by the *Viking* mission in very close approaches to the Martian moons.

Pictures of Phobos taken from as close as ninety kilometers showed thousands of fresh-looking craters. (See Figure 3-2.) The largest crater was named Stickney, which was the maiden name of Asaph Hall's wife, Angeline. It is about 10 kilometers across. This is very large, considering the small size of the moon. It is surprising that the impact of the meteoroid that created this crater did not break Phobos into little pieces. Grooves

FIGURE 3-1 *In this* Viking *orbiter photograph of Mars, the moon Phobos can be seen as a dark shadowy object toward the right of the picture. The picture was taken at an exposure proper for the brightness of Mars, which is far more reflective than its dark moons.*

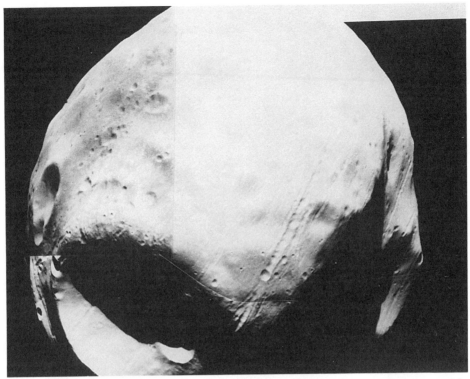

FIGURE 3-2 *The crater Stickney on Phobos. Many of the cracks and grooves on this moon may be fractures that formed during the impact that produced Stickney.*

and strings of craters that radiate away from the large crater are also visible on the surface. Features as small as 10 to 15 meters across (smaller than a typical house) can be seen in the best pictures.

In October, 1977, *Viking 2* orbiter came within 22 kilometers of the surface of Deimos. (See Figure 3-3.) Features smaller than a compact car could be seen. These included boulders and small, dust-filled craters. (See Figure 3-4.) The discovery of these little craters changed the notion that Deimos was much smoother than Phobos, as it had appeared in pictures taken from a greater distance. The dust had simply hidden the craters from view. This dust may have formed during older collisions between Deimos and meteoroids. These collisions may have thrown dust into the moon's orbit. It was eventually swept up by passage of the moon and partially filled the shallow, smaller craters.

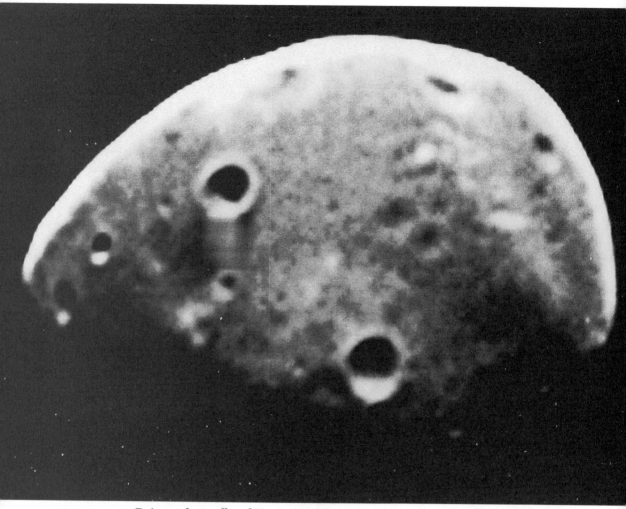

FIGURE 3-3 *Deimos, the smaller of Mars's two tiny moons. Cratered and irregular in shape, it may be a captured asteroid.*

The *Viking* orbiters also took the first color pictures of Phobos and Deimos. These pictures showed the moons to be the same dark shade of gray across their entire surfaces. Not very colorful places! The color indicates that these moons may be made up of materials called carbonaceous chondrites, which also make up some asteroids. This fact again raises the possibility that these moons, despite their nearly circular orbits, may after all have been asteroids captured at some time in the distant past.

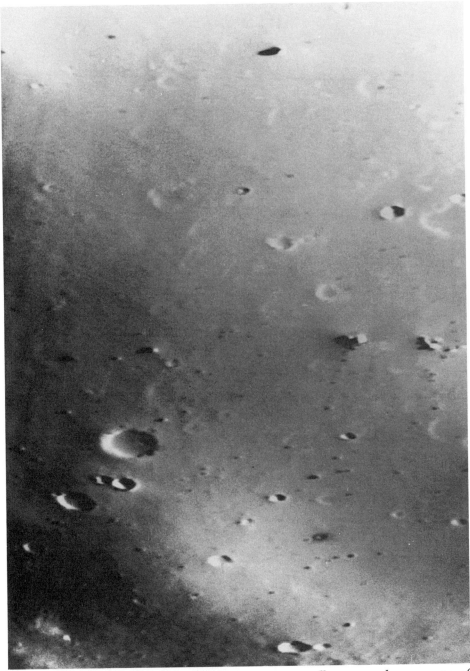

FIGURE 3-4 *At less than 50 kilometers from Deimos, many small craters can be seen, many of which are partially filled with a blanket of fine dust.*

This possibility is also supported by the fact that the moons are small. They are so small and so oddly shaped that most scientists think these moons were once part of much larger asteroids that were somehow broken apart. Sometime in the past, Phobos and Deimos may even have been part of the same asteroid. This would explain why both of them orbit directly above the equator of the planet. If the two had been captured separately, they would probably have very different orbits.

Will Phobos Collide with Mars?

Further studies of the orbit of Phobos have revealed another interesting fact. Although this moon is very small, its gravity does create tiny tides, or liftings of the surface, on Mars. The energy that causes these tides is taken from the energy of orbital motion of Phobos. This loss of energy is causing the moon to begin spiraling downward toward the surface of Mars. Within fifty million years—a short time, astronomically speaking—one of two things is likely to happen. Phobos will either fall to the surface of the planet, or else will be ripped apart by tidal forces from Mars. If it is ripped apart, a ring would be left around Mars, like the rings found around Jupiter, Saturn, and Uranus. Those who may be living on Mars at that time will likely have to deal with a heavy rain of meteorites. However, before such a breakup would occur, it might be possible to find a way to move Phobos to a safer orbit.

THE COUNTDOWN TO PHOBOS HAS BEGUN

Mars is the first planet humans are likely to colonize, since it is more like Earth than are any of the other planets of our Solar System. If you plan to be one of these pioneer colonizers, you will probably not be traveling alone. There may be many others making the trip with you, enough to establish a long-term base on Mars.

Before you land on Mars, it will make sense for you to spend some time on Phobos. Seen from there, Mars will dominate the sky, visibly seeming to move as you race about with Phobos along the moon's orbit. With this good view of Mars, you can begin to make preparations for a landing on the planet. First, you will want to decide where to land. You will keep an eye on the weather in that area of Mars, since you do not want to deal with big dust storms during your landing. You will prepare your landing vehicles and establish a small base on Phobos to relay information from Mars back to Earth. And so Phobos may become a space station, not for Martians, but for earthling travelers like you!

It may surprise you to learn that a first attempt to land on Phobos has already been made. In July, 1988, the Soviet Union launched two spacecraft, named *Phobos 1* and *Phobos 2*. Each spacecraft consisted of a Mars orbiter and smaller landers that would be dropped onto Phobos during a close encounter. One of these landers was designed to "hop" about the surface, so that many places could be studied.

Unfortunately, these missions failed. While on the way to Mars, *Phobos 1* was given a wrong command by a ground controller here on Earth. This caused it to turn around and to lose contact with Earth. *Phobos 2* continued on, reaching Mars in January, 1989. Once this craft was in orbit, its path was slowly adjusted to take it ever closer to the moon Phobos. Pictures and data were sent back, helping the controllers prepare for the landing attempts. But one of the transmitters on *Phobos 2* was no longer working, and a backup had to be used. Several other systems also showed signs of trouble. Suddenly, on March twenty-seventh, just two weeks before the spacecraft would have reached Phobos, the Soviet scientists lost contact with the craft. A week later, they proclaimed it lost.

Other attempts to reach Phobos will probably be made during the next decades. The United States is considering the possibility of assisting the Soviet Union in some of these future missions. If you should someday get to Phobos on one of these missions, you will find it a strange place. There is very little gravity, so just a gentle jump will carry you hundreds of meters. You will probably want to anchor your nearly weightless spacecraft to the surface, or the movement of the people inside might be enough to rock the craft, causing it to tip or scrape against the moon's surface. You do not want any damage to your ship to occur this far from Earth!

You may also find some useful mineral resources on Phobos, and also, eventually, on Deimos. Since the gravity of these moons is small, a great deal of energy will not be needed to send the minerals out into space on journeys to other places in the Solar System. These moons could also become major industrial centers that could produce goods useful for further exploration of the Solar System.

So, although Phobos and Deimos are among the smallest moons we know of, you can see that they are far from the least important. As is often said, good things come in small packages!

JUPITER: FORBIDDEN SMALL WORLDS

On January 31, 1958, the United States launched its first orbiting space satellite, *Explorer I.* The satellite did not visit any of the other planets or even go so far as the Moon. It did make a discovery, though, that indicated a problem that scientists will have in their explorations of Jupiter's moons.

It had long been known that Earth has a magnetic field. This field is what makes compasses work. Our planet is really like a giant magnet, with north and south magnetic poles. The magnetic poles are not quite in the same place as the northern and southern poles of rotation of the earth, but are reasonably close to them. The magnetic field traps radiation that comes from space and passes near Earth, forming high-radiation zones around our planet. These zones first showed up in measurements from *Explorer I.* They were discovered by a physicist named James Van Allen and are called the Van Allen Belts.

Spacecraft with live crews do not remain within the earth's Van Allen Belts for any extended time, since the radiation from the belts could be harmful. Jupiter poses an even greater problem. The magnetic field of the largest planet is far more powerful than that of Earth. Very dangerous radiation zones surround the planet. Any life-form that enters them without excellent protection would receive a deadly dose of radiation almost instantly. These radiation belts extend beyond the orbits of Jupiter's four largest satellites, the so-called Galilean moons.

THE GALILEANS: CALLISTO, GANYMEDE, EUROPA, AND IO

Robots and Moon Mines

Astronomers have already begun to explore the four Galilean moons of Jupiter remotely, using robot spacecraft. The *Voyager* probes gave us spectacular and awesome views of these moons. In the future, more-advanced machines may land and begin more detailed studies, even returning samples of the surface material to scientists in spacecraft safely outside the radiation zones. People may eventually use machines to mine the resources of these moons.

Even these spacecraft will have to be specially constructed to withstand the radiation. The *Voyager* spacecraft, which was not protected in this way, suffered some minor damage during its brief visit. *Galileo,* the next spacecraft to visit the Jupiter system, will pass Io, the most intensely irradiated moon, only once, in order to avoid damage to the craft's instruments.

Many science-fiction stories, and even a few movies, have depicted human explorers on the surface of the Galilean moons of Jupiter. Because of the deadly radiation belts, however, these fictional accounts will probably never be turned to fact. It seems unlikely that humans will have the chance to explore these moons. So four of the largest and potentially most useful of the moons seem to be forever locked away out of our reach. The only ways to explore them will be by machine and through our imaginations. Let us then ignore the deadly radiation and, armed with the information from the *Voyager* mission, step onto the surfaces of these exotic places.

A Great Discovery and Centuries of Mystery

The discovery of the four largest moons of Jupiter by Galileo in 1610 was one of the most important moments in the history of astronomy. Jupiter's moons were the first worlds positively shown not to be orbiting Earth. They provided the first evidence that Earth was not the center of the universe, as it was once thought to be. Their discovery also suggested that the other planets are worlds like our own and not perfect unchangeable spheres or, as had once been thought, gods patrolling the skies. Galileo suffered a great deal of persecution for his discoveries and his theories concerning them. Many people, it seemed, did not want the ancient beliefs challenged. However, it was not long before others continued the work Galileo began and made discoveries about other objects in the universe. The exploration of the skies eventually became quite a popular activity.

Despite all this exploration, however, by the time the first *Voyager* spacecraft was launched on its journey to the Galilean moons almost 370 years later, surprisingly little more had been learned about them. They were simply too small and too far away to reveal much detail to telescopes on Earth. Then, at last, the instruments of the *Voyager* spacecraft presented these worlds to us in detail, and it was as if the Solar System had magically expanded in the course of just a few days. (See Figure 4-1.) Let us now explore these four Galilean moons, starting with the outermost of them, Callisto, and proceeding inward to Ganymede, Europa, and, finally, Io.

Callisto: The Crater Capital of the Solar System

Imagine that the oceans of Earth were frozen solid. Imagine that it never rained or snowed again. Imagine further that the atmosphere of Earth disappeared and huge meteoroids began falling to the surface. This situation is similar to what we would find had occurred on Callisto.

It is a rather large moon, quite a bit larger than ours and almost as large as the planet Mercury. It is 1,885,000 kilometers from Jupiter, but is still within the radiation zones surrounding the planet. There is no atmosphere, and the temperature, nearly 800 billion kilometers from the sun, is some −150 degrees Celsius. As much as half the moon is made of ice that surrounds a rocky core. The surface then is actually an ocean of ice several hundred kilometers deep.

◄ FIGURE 4-1

The giant planet Jupiter and its four largest moons, called the Galileans. From closest to most distant in the picture, they are Callisto, Ganymede, Europa, and Io. This picture was created by combining several pictures into one. You could not see a real view like this from anywhere near Jupiter.

The early days of the Solar System marked the period of heaviest bombardment of the planets and moons by large meteoroids. These meteoroids were made up of material left over from the formation of the planets and moons. The bombardment of Callisto occurred during and after the freezing of water on that moon. It led to a great deal of cratering on the solid surfaces of Callisto, which are rough, with chunks of ice scattered about. Callisto's ice is scarred everywhere by these impacts. (See Figure 4-2 on page 56 and Color Photo 2 in the insert at the center of this book.) Each spot shows the mark of an explosive collision from the distant past. The once bright ice is now covered by dust that probably came at least partly from these impacts.

Many of Callisto's craters are rather shallow. It seems that some of the meteoroids may have broken through the surface of the moon, generating heat that partially melted some of the ice. Water would then have flowed back to fill in the basins. The rims of the craters, lifted high at formation, would have softened and slipped down toward the surface. This would occur because ice remains partly elastic—in other words, able to flow—even after refreezing. The rims of some of the oldest craters of Callisto actually seem to have moved entirely back down to the surface, leaving only faint rings behind to mark their former presence. Some craters that formed more recently have bright floors or rays extending from them. These could be made up of fresh ice uncovered in the explosive impacts that formed the craters.

Callisto—like all the other moons of Jupiter—always keeps the same face toward Jupiter. From half of the moon, Jupiter would therefore never be visible. From the other side of Callisto, it would seem to dominate the sky. If you were on that side of Callisto, Jupiter would look nearly ten times larger than the sun or Moon looks to us on Earth. However, the sun would appear to be only one fifth the size to which we are accustomed.

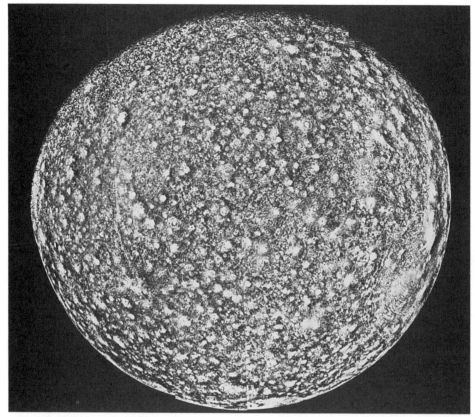

FIGURE 4-2 *This enhanced picture of Callisto clearly shows the vast number of craters covering the entire surface. Many of these craters date back to the earliest days of the Solar System, more than four billion years ago.*

Ganymede: The Planet-Sized Moon

Let us move onward to Ganymede, the biggest moon in the Solar System. Somewhat larger than the planet Mercury, it is, like Callisto, about half ice with a rocky core. The surface, though, is rather different from that of Callisto. Although regions are heavily cratered, others show a strange pattern of grooved markings. These grooves give us a hint about the surface formations on Ganymede. (See Figure 4-3 and Color Photo 3.)

As you read earlier, the period of heaviest cratering in our Solar System occurred during the first few million years of formation. Astronomers

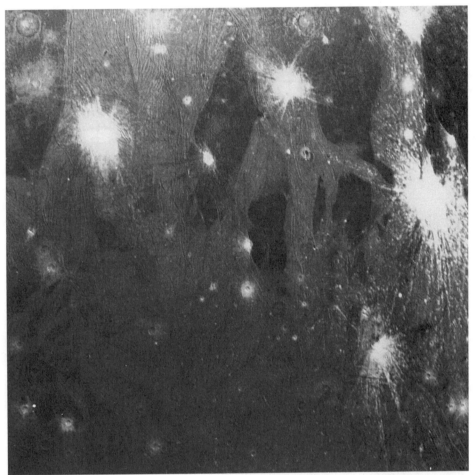

FIGURE 4-3 *This close-up of Ganymede reveals the different kinds of surfaces found on the largest moon of the Solar System. There are many craters, including apparently young ones with bright, fresh ice filling the bottoms and spreading out in rays around them. Twisting around the craters are mysterious grooves, which may indicate where the icy crust stretched and cracked as it froze billions of years ago.*

believe the water on Ganymede, unlike that on the more heavily cratered Callisto, must have frozen near the end of this time, rather than earlier. The last areas to freeze are the ones that now have the fewest craters, since few meteoroids fell to the surface after the freezing was completed. The grooves are probably caused by stretching of the surface that occurred as the water froze. Similar grooves may have formed earlier on Callisto, but would have been erased from it by the late impacts and crater formations.

Some of the grooves on Ganymede run through craters, and others lie beneath craters. Some grooves show signs of having been displaced, like fault lines on Earth, which are found where earthquakes occur. In certain places, more-recent sets of grooves on Ganymede lie over older sets, some of which are very deep. This wide variety of features makes the surface terrain a real maze that would be difficult to walk across.

Europa: Ice Fishing, Anyone?

Our next stop is Europa. Europa is just about the size of our Moon. Seen from its surface, Jupiter would appear as a huge disc in the sky, more than twenty times the size of the sun as seen from Earth. Europa's core makes up a greater portion of its volume than do the cores of Callisto or Ganymede. The surface is ice, however, like that of the other two moons.

FIGURE 4-4 *Europa is among the smoothest objects in the Solar System. This image of the full disk makes Europa look a bit like a giant Ping-Pong ball! No craters or mountains can be seen, just some cracks in the totally ice-covered world. The surface coloration may have come either from out in space or from beneath the ice.*

But, in surprising contrast to the other moons, there are almost no craters on Europa. Its worldwide ocean must have frozen after the period of heavy cratering was completely over. All in all, it is one of the smoothest worlds in the Solar System. (See Figure 4-4 on the opposite page and Color Photo 4.) There are no mountains or large canyons. If you were to explore the surface, you could use ice-skatelike devices to get around. However, you might find your journey rather dull after a while, as you skate over kilometer after endless kilometer of ice.

The frozen ocean of Europa is thought to be just slightly deeper than the oceans of Earth. If it remained liquid long enough, life may have sprung into existence in its depths, which were once warm. In fact, there may yet be a liquid ocean beneath the ice, and perhaps some simple life-forms exist there today, protected from the radiation bathing the ice above. It would be dark in those depths, but we know that some life-forms, such as those deep in our earth's oceans, do not need sunlight to survive. This idea of possible life on Europa is an interesting one, but will be very difficult to test.

If life-forms have existed for a long time on Europa, it is not impossible that intelligence might have evolved in them. Such creatures might even decide someday to try to penetrate the ice over their heads—if they have heads—and find out what lies beyond their watery "sky." If they reach the surface, radiation may kill them. But, eventually, a few of them may develop protection that would allow them to survive safely some short expeditions on the icy surface of Europa. Perhaps, if we are extremely lucky, one of our robot space probes might even stumble upon one of their expeditions!

Io: The Most Violent of Moons

Voyager 1 passed closer to Io than to any other member of Jupiter's system of worlds, coming to within 30,000 kilometers of the surface. Approaching Io, *Voyager 1* presented a view of the moon that reminded astronomers of a giant pepperoni pizza! Splotches of orange, white, red, and black mottled the surface. Features that look volcanic in origin became visible. Sulfur was seen to cover the surface. There was a complete absence of craters, which indicated to scientists that the surface of Io is probably less than one million years old and perhaps much newer than that. The landscape seemed to be still in the process of changing.

After the closest approach, the images of Io were studied more closely. Scientist Linda Moribito, checking star and moon positions in order to tell exactly where *Voyager* was as it sped through the Jupiter system, noticed a strange crescent shape near Io. She was using pictures that had been computer-processed to make details clearer. It was soon discovered that the crescent was made up of material spewing outward from an actual eruption of a volcano. Several similar features were found in other pictures. It turned out that Io was much more active volcanically than the earth. As many as nine eruptions were discovered in the *Voyager* pictures. In the four months after the passage of *Voyager 1* and before the passage of *Voyager 2,* several new changes in the surface features of Io were observed. It turns out that no specific features last long on Io. All are quickly covered by newly released volcanic material. (See Figures 4-5, 4-6, and 4-7, and Color Photos 5 and 6.)

Astronomers now believe that Io changes in this way because of a process identical to one that occurs right here on Earth: tides. The massive planet Jupiter and the other moons of the planet pull at the crust of Io. As the solid surface material slides about because of this pull, friction causes heat to build up to levels that melt the sulfur-rich material not far beneath the surface. In many places, shallow deposits of this liquid rock ooze out through cracks in the crust. Deposits of liquid sulfur that are deeper and hotter erupt in violent volcanic explosions.

As the sulfur inside Io is heated, it changes from white to orange to red. If the orange or red melted sulfur cools slowly, it can pass through these color changes in the reverse direction. If it freezes quickly, however, it may keep its warmer color. So the rate at which this fluid sulfur material freezes turns out to control the surface color on Io. In places where some of the underground heat reaches the surface, lakes of liquid sulfur of various colors may even exist for a while.

The surface of Io turns out, then, to be one of the most alien and violent places in our Solar System. If you were somehow able to stand near an erupting volcanic vent, liquid sulfur would stream upward to heights of several hundred kilometers, at which point some of the sulfur would

FIGURE 4-5 *Many spectacular views of Io were returned from* Voyager 1, *which passed within 30,000 kilometers of the strange surface. Many people describe this moon as looking like a giant pizza! Several volcanoes are visible in this picture, some of them erupting.*

freeze to form a snow of crystals. This snow falling all about you would slightly obscure your view of Jupiter itself, which would cover much of the visible sky on the side of Io facing the planet. The ground beneath you would likely shake as the eruption continued to expel the liquid sulfur. You might also observe nearby cracks in the surface from which slushy red sulfur flowed more gently out onto the surface, forming a lake that quickly froze solid. The falling sulfur snow would rapidly begin to cover the lake surface. And so, material from within Io would quickly cover and re-cover the older surface of the moon. You would be watching a world turning itself repeatedly inside out!

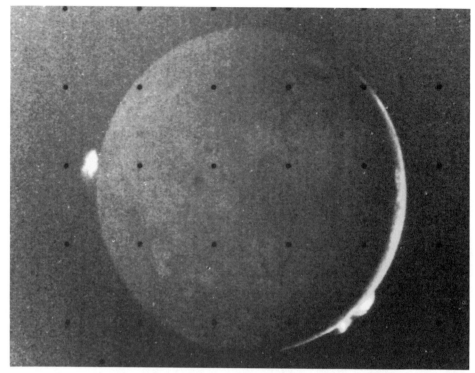

FIGURE 4-6 *It is easiest to see the eruptions of volcanoes that take place along the edge of Io. The plumes of material extend hundreds of kilometers into space.*

Some of the sulfur material that erupts from the volcanoes of Io does not fall back to the surface of the moon. It is actually blasted away at rates in excess of escape velocity. A cloud of escaped sulfur atoms, which turn into charged high-energy sulfur ions, forms a belt of material around Jupiter. This belt is known as the sulfur torus. The movement of Io through this energized torus sets up massive sparklike electrical discharges far more powerful than any lightning that occurs here on Earth. These explosive discharges also cause radio waves to be released. These waves are detectable with instruments on our planet, half a billion miles away.

Io and its space neighborhood are among the most complex and dangerous in the Solar System. We shall need very hardy robot spacecraft to explore this world successfully. The development of that sort of machine technology still lies many years in the future, however.

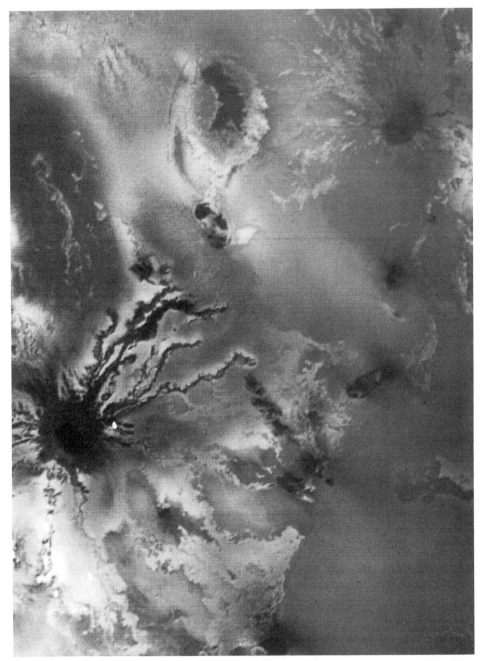

FIGURE 4-7 *This spectacular close-up of Io shows many volcanic features. These include lakes and rivers of liquid or frozen sulfur and volcanic vents through which new material oozes or sprays out onto the surface.*

THE OTHER MOONS OF JUPITER: SWARMS OF ROCKS

Besides the four Galilean satellites, Jupiter has at least a dozen smaller moons. It may once have had even more moons than it does today. Some of the vanished moons may have collided with Jupiter or been pulled away from it by the near passage of other large objects. The twelve tiny remaining worlds that have been found all have diameters less than the distance between Los Angeles and San Francisco. They are like tiny oases of matter in the sea of empty space that surrounds the massive planet.

Amalthea and Himalia: Largest of the Small

The largest of the twelve smaller moons of Jupiter are named Amalthea and Himalia. Amalthea was first seen in 1892. It is even closer to Jupiter than Io is, and, like Io, is bathed in the dangerous radiation of Jupiter. *Voyager* did get some pictures of this moon. It is potato-shaped, like the moons of Mars. Its average diameter is a little less than two hundred kilometers. It is mostly a very deep red in color. The red surface material may actually have fallen onto Amalthea after being blasted into space from the volcanoes of Io. (See Color Photo 7.)

Himalia is a heavily cratered moon similar to the moons of Mars, but about ten times larger. It is just slightly bigger than Amalthea, but is much farther from Jupiter—in fact, almost eleven and one-half million kilometers away. This is much farther than even Callisto, the most distant Galilean, which is less than two million kilometers from the planet. Himalia is safely outside the dangerous radiation belts. We might actually be able to visit it someday—that is, if we are willing to spend the time to fly to Jupiter. It took the *Voyager* spacecraft about a year and a half to travel that far.

Thebe (and Friends): Asteroid Moons

The other moons of Jupiter are smaller than Himalia, only 100 kilometers or less across. Some orbit at distances as close to Jupiter as 128,000 kilometers. Others orbit at distances as great as 23 million kilometers. Many of the moons may be captured asteroids. The dark and rocky moon Thebe is one of these. It orbits between Amalthea and Io, and is about 100 kilometers in diameter.

Metis and Andrastea: Guardians of the Ring

Jupiter is the first planet out from the sun to have a ring around it. *Voyager* cameras detected the faint ring, which is too dim to have been discovered from Earth. Most of it is extremely thin, and it actually extends all the way down to the atmosphere of Jupiter, where its particles are then captured by Jupiter itself. The ring must then get replenished by particles that come from somewhere, or else it would fade away as its particles fell into Jupiter. Possibly the volcanoes of Io provide the materials that make up the ring.

The two innermost moons of Jupiter may also have something to do with the ring. One of them, Metis, orbits just inside the primary part of the ring. The other, Andrastea, orbits just outside. Though very small—less than 40 kilometers across—these two moons may be helping to stabilize a portion of the ring, allowing its particles to remain in orbit. In this way, the ring can continue to exist without a constant input of large quantities of material.

Ananke, Carme, Pasiphae, and Sinope: The Far Outposts

The four outermost moons of Jupiter—Ananke, Carme, Pasiphae, and Sinope—are more than 20 million kilometers from the planet. Their orbits are strange and interesting. They are far more elongated than the orbits of the inner moons. Also, the orbital motion of these four moons is opposite in direction to that of the other moons. These facts support the idea that many of the moons of Jupiter may be captured asteroids. It is also possible that some, if not all, of the four outermost moons originally came from one larger "parent" asteroid that broke up and formed them.

Leda, Lysithea, and Elara: A Polar View of Jupiter

Another group of moons—Leda, Lysithea, and Elara (together with Himalia, which you read about earlier)—have unusual orbits. Though these moons revolve around the planet in the same direction as the inner moons, their orbits are not in the same plane. They are inclined by 25 – 29 degrees and lie about 11 million kilometers from Jupiter. From the surface of one of these, we would be able to study the polar regions of Jupiter better than we would from a moon orbiting directly above the equator. Again, most likely the moons are captured asteroids.

As you have seen, the small worlds that orbit Jupiter are certainly fascinating. However, many are too dangerous for humans to explore. So, sadly, the spacecraft that will eventually explore these moons will probably not contain human crews. As we collect more information, however, we shall be able to take more and more rewarding imaginary expeditions to these forbidden, distant small worlds.

SATURN: RINGS AND MOONS

Very few people have talked seriously about ever making a visit to Jupiter, the planet you read about in the last chapter. Since most of its interesting moons are too dangerous to visit because of the radiation belts discussed earlier, there is little to tempt anyone out that far. However, the moons of the planet Saturn offer the possibility of much adventure, with much less danger, if we someday find a way to reach that distant world. There are radiation belts around Saturn, but they are not nearly as intense as those of Jupiter. Saturn has plenty of moons worth visiting. One of them, Titan, is different from any of the other known moons of our Solar System in at least one very important way.

SATURN'S SEVENTEEN MOONS—OR MAYBE TWENTY-THREE?

Most of Saturn's moons had been discovered from Earth before *Voyager*

1 and *Voyager 2* passed near Saturn in 1980 and 1981. These space probes photographed a number of new moons. There were indications of still other moons in some of the scientific studies that were done. There may be anywhere from seventeen to twenty-three moons orbiting Saturn—the most in the Solar System.

TITAN: THE BEST MOON OF THEM ALL

It would be easy to become sad and lonely far from family and friends on Earth. Homesickness would be a major problem to be solved in space exploration. To explore the outer Solar System effectively, we would probably have to establish a major base somewhere, with pleasant conditions to keep courageous pioneers happy.

Titan, one of the moons of Saturn, might make a good place to build such a base. Titan is the largest of Saturn's moons. It is very large—just a little smaller than Jupiter's largest, Ganymede. However, it has a major advantage over that moon and probably any other as well. It is the only moon that we are certain has an atmosphere whose density is as great as that of Earth. (See Figure 5-1.) In fact, *Voyager* data indicated that the atmospheric density of Titan is even greater than that of the earth—more than one and one-half times greater, to be precise. Titan's atmosphere is made up mostly of nitrogen, the same gas that makes up 78 percent of the air we breathe. However, Titan is very different from Earth in one important regard. It is about ten times farther from the sun, and is therefore very cold, about – 180 degrees Celsius. You would have to be very fond of wintry weather to want to live there!

What? Smog on a Moon?

It has not been possible to tell exactly what the surface of Titan is like, even though *Voyager 1* flew within just 5 thousand kilometers of this moon in November of 1980. Titan is entirely covered by a cloud of orange "smog." (See Figure 5-2.) This smoglike material is created by the breakdown of methane molecules, which make up about 3 percent of the atmosphere, by ultraviolet radiation from the sun. Some of the gases produced by this breakdown condense to form the tiny smog particles.

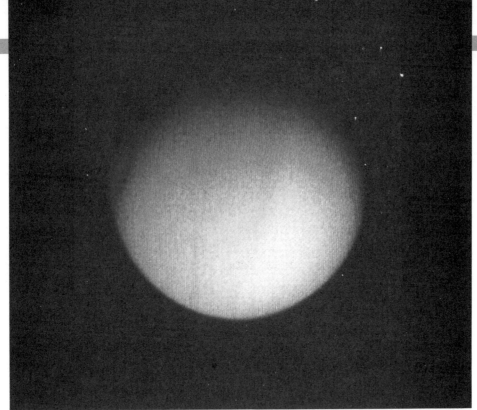

FIGURE 5-1 *Titan is the largest moon of Saturn and the only moon with a significant atmosphere. No surface features can be seen because the atmosphere is filled with a smog of orange particles produced by complex chemical reactions.*

FIGURE 5-2 *Sunlight can be seen shining through Titan's smoglike atmosphere from behind and revealing the entire disk of the moon.*

These gases include ethane, acetylene, ethylene, and, most importantly, hydrogen cyanide. This latter gas is one whose presence is generally believed by scientists to have made possible the origin of life on Earth. Its presence on Titan does not mean that we expect to find life on that moon, however. There is something very important missing on Titan, and that is oxygen. On Earth, much of the oxygen came from water vapor, but any water on Titan is frozen solid and is unlikely to evaporate extensively. If water vapor could be released into Titan's atmosphere, it might react with the hydrogen cyanide that is already there and begin the process that could lead toward the development of life.

Many scientists think that Titan is covered by an orange residue of smog particles that have fallen to the ground. This covering of residue could be as much as a kilometer deep. Below the residue, there is probably a layer of methane, ammonia, and water ices that is roughly 800 kilometers thick and that makes up about half the mass of Titan. Below the ice, there is probably a rocky core.

However, some scientists have a different theory about Titan's surface. They believe that the surface of Titan may be liquid. They suggest that the very low temperatures could make methane behave much the way water does here on Earth, existing in liquid form, as well as vapor and solid forms. In fact, they claim that we might someday find that an ocean of liquid methane covers much of Titan.

Resources on Titan

If we could reach Titan—and could find enough solid land to build a base—there would be plenty of useful resources available there. The methane could be burned to supply heat energy. Water could be recovered from the assorted ices found on the surface or be mined from beneath the covering of smog particles. The water could then be used in greenhouses for the growth of needed plants, which would supply both food and oxygen. Moving around on Titan would not be very hard, since surface gravity would be slightly less, even, than that on our Earth's Moon. The presence of all that smog would be unfortunate, however. Imagine the view we could have of Saturn's nearby fantastic rings if only the sky over Titan would clear.

Days on Titan would be rather long. It takes this moon almost sixteen Earth days to orbit Saturn, and, like most other moons, Titan keeps the same face toward its parent planet as it revolves. So its day is sixteen Earth days long. This might not make a great deal of difference, however, since the distant sun never lights up the skies very brightly. Only a dim orange light filters through, making it look like sunset even in the middle of the day.

Of all the places beyond Earth here in our Solar System, there are few that offer the size, resources, and relative safety that Titan does. As you have read, it is large, has reasonable gravity, and has a dense and useful atmosphere. Given the distance of Titan, however, human settlement there may not take place for quite a long time.

HYPERION, IAPETUS, AND PHOEBE:
THE SUBURBS OF SATURN

Most of the other moons of Saturn are closer to the planet than Titan is. This places them deeper in Saturn's magnetic field, and so they are likely to receive more radiation. There are, however, three known moons that are more distant than Titan and that would be less dangerous to visit—at least as far as radiation is concerned. The first of them, Hyperion, is about 1.5 million kilometers from Saturn. Iapetus is about 3.5 million kilometers out, and Phoebe nearly 13 million. Each of these is interesting for one reason or another.

Hyperion: The Tumbling Moon

Hyperion is rather small, about 250 kilometers across. It is not spherical, however. In fact, it is rather flattened and pitted, and looks something like a beat-up hamburger patty! It does not keep the same face toward Saturn, but actually seems to be in a tumbling rotation along its orbit. Its rate of rotation changes over time, which is not the case for any other known world in our Solar System.

Something strange must have happened to this moon. Many astronomers believe that Hyperion may originally have been a larger, spherical moon. A collision or series of collisions with other moons, asteroids, or meteoroids near Saturn may have broken away pieces of the original Hyperion. What we see today is probably just a battered remnant of the ancient moon. (See Figure 5-3.) The collisions also may be responsible for the fact that Hyperion does not keep the same face toward Saturn. The force of the impacts would have added plenty of energy to the rotation of this moon, not allowing it to become locked gravitationally to its parent planet. The gravity of the moon Titan may also be affecting Hyperion's rotation, possibly causing the variation in the speed at which Hyperion turns.

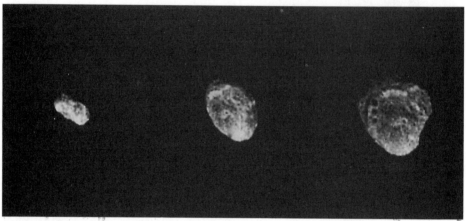

FIGURE 5-3 *Three views of Hyperion, a moon that appears to have suffered many collisions with other objects. These collisions broke off pieces that drifted away millions of years ago. The moon still rotates in a strange fashion as a result of the ancient impacts.*

Iapetus: Two Moons in One

Iapetus, one of the larger moons of Saturn, is nearly 1,500 kilometers across. Since its discovery in 1671, it has been one of the most mysterious moons of the Solar System. Long ago, observers noticed that the moon varies a great deal in brightness as it orbits the planet. One half of the moon turns out for some reason to be much brighter than the other. (See Figure 5-4 and Color Photo 8.) In his novel *2001: A Space Odyssey,* Arthur C. Clarke explained this by presenting Iapetus as a world altered by an alien race to service as an invitation for humans to visit their civilization. Unfortunately, perhaps, *Voyager* images of this moon did not indicate anything like that had happened. Neither did they provide enough information to allow scientists to solve completely the mystery of the moon's two faces.

The pictures from *Voyager* were detailed enough to show us some of the features in the bright hemisphere, which is rather sharply separated from the dark side. Studies of Iapetus's spectrum indicate that this bright hemisphere is made up of ice. The fact that the mass of this moon is low for its size suggests further that the interior of the moon is mostly ice as well.

The dark side of Iapetus is difficult to see in the *Voyager* pictures, as the light was not strong enough to show details clearly. The material on this dark side was already known to be only one tenth as bright as that on the icy side of the moon. Since the moon is probably made up mostly of ice, the dark material was assumed to make up only a thin layer covering

FIGURE 5-4 *One of the strangest moons of the Solar System, Iapetus displays two very different sides: one very bright, the other among the darkest observed anywhere. Scientists do not yet know whether the dark material comes from within Iapetus or from out in space.*

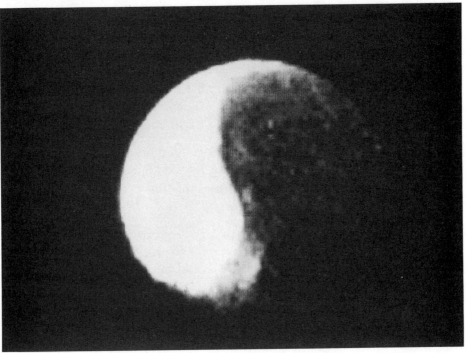

bright ice. However, there is a problem with that assumption. If it were correct, astronomers should see bright craters in the dark area, since a thin covering could be removed by impacts that would expose the brighter subsurface ice. There were no bright craters seen, however. This only intensified the mystery of the origin and nature of the dark material.

The dark hemisphere is known to face in the direction of Iapetus's orbit about Saturn. Some astronomers believe that the dark material may be dust continuously swept up by the moon as it moves through space. This dark dust may quickly cover up any exposed ice. However, there may be a problem with this theory as well. There are indications that the crater floors are more heavily saturated with the black material than is the rest of the dark hemisphere. If the dark dust comes from space, it should instead cover the new crater surfaces less thickly, rather than more thickly. Other scientists have come up with yet another theory to account for the dark material. They think that it may ooze up from beneath the surface of Iapetus. It will be difficult to resolve all these mysteries unless we someday send a spacecraft that can gather samples of Iapetus's dark coating and discover what it is made of.

Phoebe: A Dusty Wayward Intruder

Phoebe is a moon whose origin is very much in question. It has an orbit that is more elliptical than that of Saturn's other moons. Even more interesting, it is revolving around Saturn in the direction opposite from that of the other moons. It is quite dark and appears to be more rocky than icy, which is also very unusual for moons in this part of the Solar System. These facts suggest strongly that Phoebe is a captured asteroid.

Some astronomers have offered theories that Phoebe may be the source of the surface material on the dark side of Iapetus. Small meteoroids striking the surface of Phoebe (which is a rather small moon, only about 220 kilometers across) could propel dust into the space around Saturn. Iapetus, the moon nearest to Phoebe, would be the first small world to encounter this dust and may sweep it up before it reaches other satellites. All this assumes that the dark material comes to Iapetus from space. As you have just seen, however, there are problems with that assumption as well. Thus, the mysteries of Iapetus and Phoebe continue unresolved.

ON THE WAY IN TOWARD THE RINGS

The moons of Saturn that travel inside the orbit of the moon Titan are among the most complex bodies in the Solar System. (See Figure 5-5.) Not only do they have a multitude of surface features, such as cracks, craters, ice, and rocks, but they provide examples of some very complicated principles of orbital motion.

FIGURE 5-5 *This collection of pictures shows many of the smaller inner moons of Saturn seen by the* Voyager 2 *spacecraft. These moons seem similar to Phobos and Deimos, the moons of Mars, and may be captured asteroids.*

Rhea: Another Two-Faced Moon

First we come to Rhea, a little over one-half million kilometers from Saturn. (See Figures 5-6 and 5-7.) It is slightly larger than Iapetus, and it also has contrasting bright and dark hemispheres. In the case of Rhea, however, the bright side, rather than the dark one, faces the direction of orbit. The dark side of Rhea appears to have more-complex surface features than does its bright side, which is fairly smooth. Rhea is made up mostly of ice, so it is possible that some process may have partially melted the surface of the bright leading edge of this moon, allowing the craters and other features to melt away on that side.

FIGURE 5-6 *The surface of Rhea. Craters upon craters dot the landscape.*

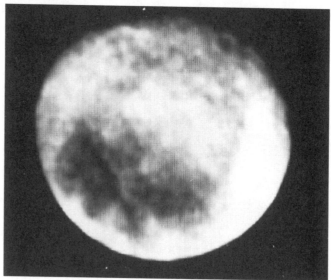

FIGURE 5-7 *Rhea appears splotched with patches of bright ice. Tidal forces may be melting subsurface ice that flows out to cover the ancient landscape.*

Dione: A Moon with a Moon

At a distance of 380,000 kilometers, we encounter Dione, which is a bit smaller than Rhea but similar in appearance. (See Figure 5-8 and Color Photo 9.) The unusual fact about Dione is that another moon shares the same orbit with it. The other moon is very small, only about 30 kilometers in diameter. At the time of its discovery, it was designated simply as 1980S6 (since it was the sixth moon of Saturn discovered in 1980). It has since been given the name Helene.

Helene is sixty degrees, or one sixth of an orbit, ahead of Dione. This degree of separation is a critical one. Orbiting bodies in such relative

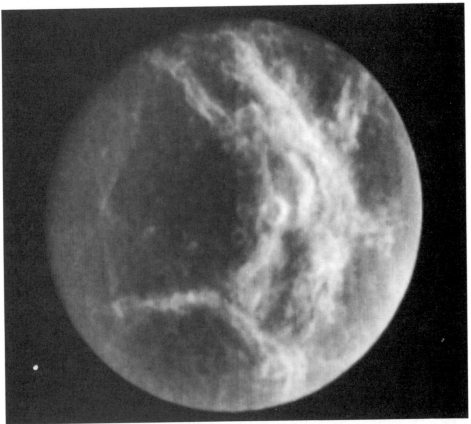

FIGURE 5-8 *In this picture, Dione appears heavily cratered and streaked with deposits of ice. The surface ice may indicate some type of internal activity generating heat that melts internal water. This water could seep out through cracks in the surface and then freeze.*

positions are on what are known as Lagrangian points, which are named for a French mathematician who discovered them. They arise because of the interaction of gravity between two such bodies and the body they orbit. At Lagrangian points, gravitational forces, in effect, cancel each other. An orbiting body placed at one does not move toward either of the other two bodies. The relative positions of the bodies are stable. Since Helene is located at one of the stable Lagrangian points in the Saturn–Dione system, it will remain ahead of Dione, in the same orbit and at the same distance. There is no danger of a collision between the two moons unless some outside force enters the picture.

Tethys: A Moon with Two Moons

The next moon in toward Saturn, at 295,000 kilometers from the planet, is Tethys. (See Figure 5-9 and Color Photo 10.) It is very similar to Dione in size. One of the main differences between the two is the presence of a huge crater on Tethys, one that is much larger than any found on Dione. There is also a giant crack that is roughly 100 kilometers wide, 1,000 kilometers long, and 2 kilometers deep. It probably formed as the ice at the core of Tethys froze and expanded, splitting the long-frozen crust above. Tethys has two Lagrangian satellites sharing its orbit, one sixty degrees ahead of it and another sixty degrees behind it. They are called Calypso and Telesto. They are extremely small moons, less than twenty-five kilometers across.

Enceladus: A Moon like a Mirror

At a distance of 238,000 kilometers from Saturn, we find Enceladus. This moon is one of the most highly reflective objects in the Solar System. (See Color Photo 11.) Nearly 100 percent of the sunlight that reaches its surface is bounced back into space. This 500-kilometer-wide ball of ice is also interesting because it has fewer craters than do most of the moons of Saturn. Astronomers believe that some form of geologic activity must be going on to keep the surface as smooth as it is. Tidal forces caused by Saturn and some of the large moons may produce heat beneath the surface and bring about the geologic activity.

FIGURE 5-9 *The two moons Tethys and Dione in orbit around Saturn. The magnificent ring system of Saturn and the giant planet itself make the moons look rather insignificant. The rings themselves represent billions of additional tiny "moons" of Saturn—chunks of rock and ice all independently orbiting this beautiful world.*

Mimas: Bashed and Broken

Passing inside the extremely thin outermost ring of Saturn, we approach Mimas. This world appears to be among the most battered in the Solar System. One of its craters extends roughly one quarter around its 390-kilometer diameter. (See Figure 5-10 and Color Photo 12.) Many scientists believe that if the object that struck Mimas and created this crater had been only a little bigger, it would have shattered the moon. There is a theory that suggests that at one time Mimas actually was broken up into chunks that continued to orbit Saturn until they fell back together and were compressed to re-form the moon we see today. This shattering and re-forming may have even been repeated several times!

FIGURE 5-10 *Large cracks may have formed on Mimas when the large impact that caused this moon's giant crater occurred. Many small craters are visible in this picture.*

Janus and Epimetheus: The Dancing Moons

At a distance of 150,000 kilometers from Saturn, we find the strangest pair of satellites in the Solar System. They are also the largest of Saturn's irregular rocky (as opposed to icy) moons. Janus and Epimetheus, 190 and 120 kilometers across, respectively, are referred to as the co-orbitals. This is because they are very close together as they orbit Saturn. Actually, at any given moment, one or the other of the two is slightly closer to Saturn than is its companion. This moon therefore moves slightly faster during this period and begins to catch up with the other one. As the two approach, their gravity causes them to carry out an exotic dancelike motion. In the process of the dance, they switch places. The other moon then becomes the satellite that is closer to Saturn and faster moving. When the two next meet again, the dance is repeated. Standing on one of these two worlds as its "dancing partner" approaches might be quite frightening. You might think they were about to collide!

THE RINGS: STONES, SNOWBALLS, AND BRAIDED BANDS

We are now approaching the main ring system of Saturn. It is, of course, the feature that most obviously identifies this planet. Through Earth telescopes, the rings appear to be made up of just three mistlike main sections with gaps between them. Even the very best Earth-based pictures until recently revealed no further details. The rings are named A, B, and C, the A ring being the one of these that is farthest from the planet. The largest and most easily seen gap is the Cassini division, which separates the A and B rings. A smaller gap, called the Encke division, is embedded within the A ring. The B and C rings are not separated by a gap, but it is easy to tell them apart. The B ring is large and bright, whereas the C ring is quite dim. Another ring, designated D and located inside the C ring, was not discovered until the 1960s. In 1966, when the ring system was visible edge-on from the earth, the very faint E ring was seen for the first time. It lies far outside the other rings.

In 1979, the spacecraft *Pioneer 11* passed near Saturn. The pictures it sent back were only slightly better than those available from Earth, but still another ring, called the F ring, was detected slightly beyond the A ring.

Then came *Voyager*. As the first of the twin spacecraft approached the planet in November, 1980, our beliefs about the misty nature of the rings began to change. It was discovered that, instead, thousands of "ringlets" make up each of the main ring bands. Some were visible even in the former gaps. At close range, the rings seemed to resemble a giant, multicolored grooved phonograph record! So it turns out that the famous rings

FIGURE 5-11 *Detailed image of Saturn's rings. If we were to count each of its ring particles as a moon, Saturn would have billions of moons!*

of Saturn are not continuous; in other words, you would not be able to walk all the way around Saturn on a ring. Instead, within each ring billions of pieces of rock and ice follow their own individual orbits about the planet. (See Figure 5-11.) A ring can be thought of as a band of tiny moons.

One of the great challenges that face astronomers is to determine how the rings maintain their complex structure. Most theories seem to indicate that the rings should slowly disintegrate, the material in them drifting closer to the planet. However, this does not appear to be happening.

Most puzzling of all is the F ring. During the passage of the *Voyager 1* spacecraft, two separate braided strands were found to make up this ring. There were also some signs of a faint third strand slightly inside the orbit of the braided pair. These features present a baffling problem, as no known process seems able to explain their existence.

THE INNERMOST MOONS OF SATURN

All of the Saturnian moons that you have read about so far lie well beyond the planet's main rings. The remaining ones—Pandora, Prometheus, Atlas, and a few others—do not. As you will see, the presence of these moons may partly explain some of the strange characteristics of the rings.

Pandora and Prometheus: The Shepherd Moons

Saturn's mysterious F ring turns out to be straddled on each side by moons, called 1980S26 and 1980S27 and also known as Pandora and Prometheus. Although each is barely 100 kilometers in diameter, the gravity of these two satellites influences the F ring. Their presence may explain how this ring keeps its structure without drifting toward the planet and disintegrating. For this reason, these two moons are often referred to as the shepherd moons. They "shepherd" the particles in the ring and help to hold the ring together.

It was thought that the presence of these moons might also explain the braiding of the F ring that had been observed by *Voyager 1*. However, by the time *Voyager 2* arrived one year later, the F ring was no longer braided. The mystery of the presence of the braids was gone, but only to be replaced by the mystery of their sudden absence. There is no explanation yet as to why the braiding disappeared. We shall need to study the F ring and its two shepherd moons more closely on another space mission in order to try to find the answer.

Atlas (and Company): Midget Moons

One more moon has been positively identified within Saturn's ring system. Tiny Atlas is just thirty kilometers across and orbits just outside the A ring, 137,000 kilometers from the planet. Its gravity, though feeble, may be enough to help shepherd the particles of the A ring.

There were faint indications of between three and six other Saturnian moons in photographs taken by the *Voyager* spacecraft. These moons have not been located with enough certainty to allow scientists to establish their orbits, however.

As you have seen, the satellites of Saturn offer us an exciting assortment of places to study in the future. They may someday reveal more of the secrets of planetary and satellite motion and ring formation. Best of all, one of them, the big moon Titan, may be used to set up scientific bases for study of the outer Solar System. Though Saturn and its moons are distant worlds, no doubt they will be of great interest to the space explorers of the future.

6
URANUS:
HOME OF SURPRISING
MOONS

After visiting Jupiter and Saturn, the *Voyager 2* spacecraft moved on toward its next major destination: distant Uranus, the seventh planet from the sun. In January of 1986, some years after passing Saturn, *Voyager* finally reached Uranus. Its overall journey from Earth—more than eight years long—had not been easy. Near Jupiter, the craft had been bathed in fierce radiation. It barely survived a dangerous plunge through the ring plane of Saturn, where it might easily have collided with ring particles that would have smashed it to bits. By the time it reached Uranus, many of the instruments it carried had become unreliable, and a few had broken down completely. And yet, *Voyager 2* would perform in spectacular fashion its mission to Uranus. It would send back much information about that planet and its moons—information that would show that even the outer reaches of the Solar System are varied, fascinating, and full of surprises.

A NEW CHALLENGE FOR *VOYAGER*

Visiting Uranus was different from visiting the other planets. There were new problems. At almost three billion kilometers from the sun, the light levels were much lower than at Jupiter or Saturn. This meant that in order to get detailed and bright pictures, the cameras on *Voyager 2* had to take long time exposures. Since the probe was then moving at about fifteen kilometers per second, the long exposures might result in blurred pictures. A way would have to be found to move the camera so as to make up for the movement of the spacecraft. This took a great deal of special program-ming of the computer on *Voyager,* but it worked very well.

Another problem to be solved arose from an unusual feature of the Uranian system. The axis of the planet is greatly tilted compared to that of the other planets. It is nearly parallel to the orbital plane. This means that the planet is, in a sense, tipped on its side. Its polar areas point almost directly toward the sun during their summer and directly away during their winter. In fact, because of the eighty-four-year orbital period of Uranus, each pole is entirely in the dark for more than twenty years at a time during its long winter.

The moons of Uranus orbit the planet about its equator, like the moons of the other planets. Because of the planet's tilt, however, the orbits do not lie in the plane of the solar system, but at almost right angles to it. The Uranian system would then look something like a circular dart board from the approaching *Voyager*'s point of view. The planet would lie at the bull's-eye and the orbits of the moons would form the rings around it. As *Voyager 2* approached Uranus, it would fly closest to all of the moons at about the same time. In the case of the other, less tilted planets, *Voyager* had encountered moons basically one by one: first the outer moons on the near side, then the inner moons, and then the outer moons on the far side, as it passed a planet and moved away. At Uranus, *Voyager* would not have time for such leisurely study. The spacecraft would have to change its camera targets rapidly in order to see at least something of all the moons.

On January 24, 1986, *Voyager* made its closest approach to Uranus. Most of the pictures of the largest moons were taken on that day and the one following. These photographs provided many of the greatest surprises of the entire *Voyager* mission so far. But, before you read about this new information, you need to find out what was known about the moons of Uranus before *Voyager* reached that planet.

THE SOLAR SYSTEM GROWS BY ONE PLANET AND FIVE MOONS

Uranus was officially discovered by William Herschel in 1781. Actually, the planet probably had been seen before, as it is barely visible to the naked eye. Herschel, however, was the first to recognize it as a planet. This discovery was very significant, since the orbit of Uranus was so large that the known Solar System doubled in size with the discovery.

Six years later, Herschel discovered two Uranian moons, Titania and Oberon. In 1851, William Lassell discovered two more, Umbriel and Ariel.

FIGURE 6-1 *Oberon is splashed with cratered plains and streaked with ice. A large mountain can be seen projecting from the rim of this moon, near the lower-left edge of the photo.*

Finally, in 1948, Gerard P. Kuiper discovered another, Miranda. The five moons ranged in size from less than 500 kilometers across (Miranda) to about 1,600 kilometers across (Titania). At their great distance from Earth, they were extremely faint and little could be learned about them. Their orbits indicated that their masses were low for their size. Therefore, the moons were assumed to be composed mostly of water ice. No atmosphere was detected around any of them.

The chance *Voyager* gave us to see this distant system of moons was exciting, but most astronomers did not expect to find very interesting worlds. They thought they would find surfaces that had changed very little in the low-temperature conditions. Any heat originally present in the small moons was assumed to have been lost long ago. Geologic processes such as volcanoes or earthquakes were therefore thought to be unlikely. In short, the astronomers expected to observe heavily cratered worlds similar to our Moon in appearance and basically unchanged for billions of years.

THE FIVE MAJOR MOONS OF URANUS

Oberon: Craters Splashed with Muddy Water

Oberon was the first moon to begin to reveal its detail to the *Voyager* cameras. (See Figure 6-1.) Craters became visible. From many of them extended bright rays like those we see around some of the craters of our Moon. However, the astronomers also noticed dark areas inside the craters. These appeared to be signs of eruption. Muddy water had splashed outward onto the surface through cracks. This was not at all expected, as it indicated that there was activity inside the moon. The Uranian system had revealed the first of its surprises.

Titania: Giant Cracks

Voyager revealed giant canyonlike cracks on the moon Titania that were at first puzzling. (See Figure 6-2.) Astronomers now think they know what may have caused these cracks. As water freezes, it expands. Since Titania is mostly water, its interior expanded when it began to freeze. The

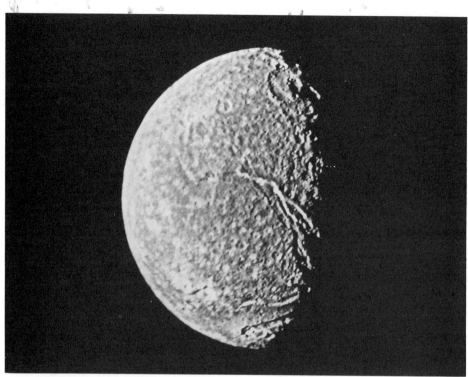

FIGURE 6-2 *A thousand-kilometer-long valley can be seen in this image of Titania, the largest moon of Uranus.*

expansion cracked the surface. The cracks are thought to be billions of years old.

Titania's surface is marked by craters, but mysteriously few of them are large. This may be related to the fact that this moon is the largest of the moons of Uranus. When the young moon first began to cool in the early days of the Solar System, it was, like all moons its age, heavily bombarded by large meteoroids. Such impacts would have generated more heat in the interior of Titania than they did in smaller moons, which, because of their weaker gravity, attracted fewer meteoroids. This large amount of heat may have partially melted Titania once again, so that the larger craters that formed early disappeared into the molten surface. Only the newer craters, which were typically formed by smaller meteoroids, are still present today.

Umbriel: Dark Craters and a Mysterious Bright Ring

Even before the *Voyager* visit, it was known that Umbriel was the darkest of the Uranian moons. Astronomers had expected that this unusual darkness would, on closer examination, reveal itself to have been caused by interesting processes. Most of the astronomers suspected that smooth lava fields caused by volcanoes accounted for the darkness. Instead, the *Voyager* pictures showed almost nothing on Umbriel but dark craters. Umbriel turned out to have a surface older than that of Oberon or Titania. It was the first Uranian moon to show the ancient cratered surface that *Voyager* scientists had expected to be typical of the moons of Uranus.

However, there was also a mysterious bright ring that seemed to lie within one of Umbriel's craters. (See Figure 6-3.) This ring is now thought to be an ice deposit formed when water from far below reached the frigid surface of the moon. The water could have been released when a large

FIGURE 6-3 *Except for the floor of one crater seen near the top of this image, Umbriel is darker than the other moons of Uranus. The crater may be a fairly new one whose creation has exposed fresh ice.*

meteoroid struck Umbriel and formed a deep crater as it blasted through outer dark material overlaying ice fields. It is a mystery to astronomers why such a thing should have happened in only one place on this moon. In any case, the bright ring feature must be a relatively recent addition to the surface of Umbriel. By *recent,* we mean only about a million years old!

Ariel: A Canyon World

The next target of the *Voyager* cameras was Ariel, a moon that (like the previous three) was much smaller than Earth. The *Voyager* scientists had assumed that Ariel had cooled very quickly long ago and would not show any signs of geologic activity. Well, they were wrong again! Giant canyons, with smooth, flat floors, stretched all about the visible surface of Ariel. (See Figures 6-4 and 6-5.) It appeared that these canyons had been cut by a liquid or a soft ice that had flowed across this moon. The liquid could not have been water, which would have been in a frozen state on this world. Some other substance, such as methane, ammonia, or carbon monoxide, possibly mixed with water, may have been soft enough to form these features. Gravitational tidal forces caused by Uranus and some of the other moons may have created the heat necessary to make this substance fluid enough to flow.

Miranda: The Strangest of All Moons

Voyager 2 passed closer to Miranda than it did to any of the other Uranian satellites. (See Figure 6-6 and Color Photo 13.) Scientists assumed that, since Miranda was the smallest of the major moons, it was likeliest of all of them to turn out to be just a heavily cratered ancient rock. Once again, they were wrong.

Although some areas on the surface of Miranda do look like the ancient cratered highlands of our own Moon, Miranda showed at least as much variety as any other moon yet visited in the Solar System. (See Figures 6-8 and 6-9.) Its equator is flanked by twin oval features made up of grooves resembling a racetrack. Near its south pole, there is a feature that looks like a giant checkmark. There is a cliff nearby that is almost twenty kilometers high—that is more than twice as high as Everest, Earth's tallest mountain. It would take an object or person almost ten minutes to fall to

FIGURE 6-4 *Ariel is deeply faulted, probably because of a long history of violent impacts and because of its fragile, icy composition.*

FIGURE 6-5 *Ariel is small but covered with craters and cracks.*

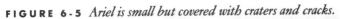

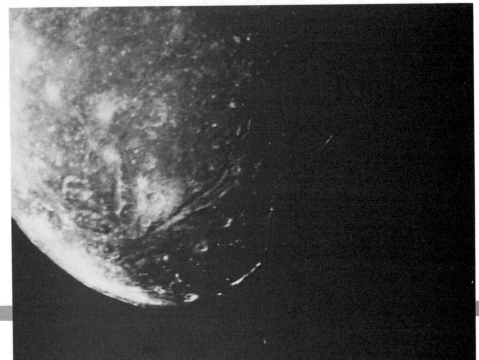

FIGURE 6-6 *The spacecraft* Voyager 2 *as it may have appeared near Uranus's moon Miranda. This spacecraft has visited more worlds than any other in history.*

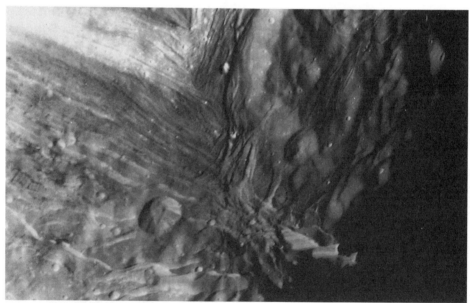

FIGURE 6-7 *A close-up view of the tortured surface of Miranda. In the lower-right corner is a cliff some 20 kilometers high. It would take nearly 10 minutes for an object dropped over its edge to reach the bottom!*

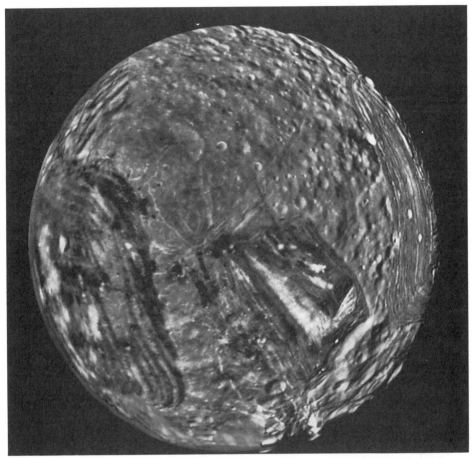

FIGURE 6-8 *This full-disk composite of many pictures of Miranda displays the many different features that make this moon one of the most interesting in the Solar System.*

the bottom of this giant cliff, given the very low gravity of Miranda. (See Figure 6-7.)

Scientists have proposed a possible overall explanation for the strange features of this moon. It seems quite likely that, early in the Solar System's development, Miranda was subject to collisions with meteoroid bodies large enough to break the moon into pieces. These pieces gradually came back together again, to re-form the moon. The features we see today are indications of the violence of the forces that acted in earlier times in our Solar System.

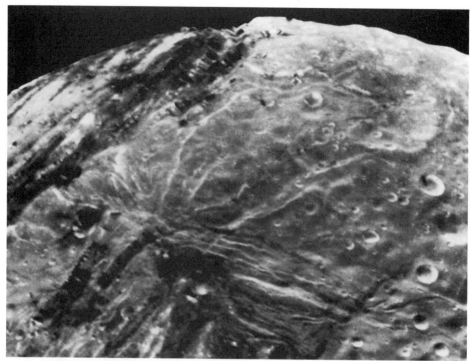

FIGURE 6-9 *This close-up of Miranda against a black background of space shows an extremely rugged terrain.*

THE NEWEST MEMBERS OF THE URANIAN SYSTEM

The five moons discussed so far were found many years ago. Ten new Uranian moons were found by *Voyager*. All of them are much smaller than the original five. The largest, known as Puck, is heavily cratered and extremely dark. It is barely 170 kilometers across. Puck was the only moon discovered in 1985. The other nine moons, in order of their discovery, are Portia, Juliet, Cressida, Rosalind, Belinda, Desdemona, Cordelia, Ophelia, and Bianca. (Some of the names may sound familiar; all but one come from characters in the plays of Shakespeare.) The smallest of the moons, Cordelia, is only 40 kilometers wide. These nine small moons were not found until *Voyager*'s closest encounter with the planet. In the pictures taken of them, they appear simply as tiny dots. (See Figure 6-10.)

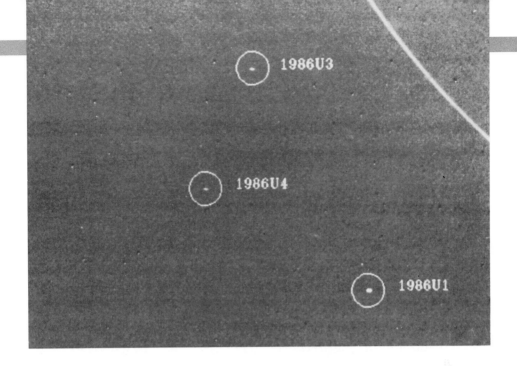

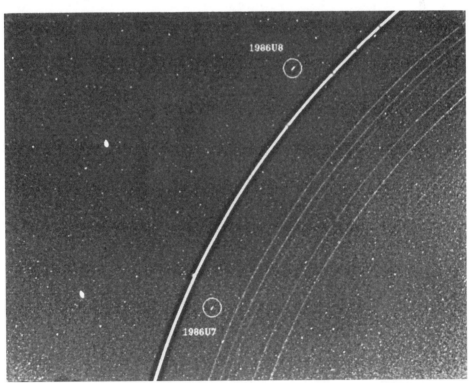

FIGURE 6-10 *These two pictures show five of the tiny moons of Uranus discovered by* Voyager 2 *in January, 1986. 1986U8 and 1986U7—now renamed Ophelia and Cordelia—are "shepherd" moons that help guide ring material around Uranus.*

All of the ten new moons orbit inside the paths of the larger five. Their orbits are quite close together, at roughly 60,000 to 70,000 kilometers from the planet. It is possible that the moons originated as a single larger body that has been broken up into smaller pieces.

Two of the newly discovered moons—Cordelia and Ophelia—are interesting because of their importance to another feature of Uranus, its rings. These rings, which were discovered in 1977, are not nearly as impressive as those of Saturn, being smaller, less dense, and darker. At least ten of them have been found around Uranus, including the faintest, which was discovered by *Voyager*. It is possible that the material that makes them up came from the original large moon that may have broken up to form the ten smallest Uranian moons. In any case, the moons Cordelia and Ophelia were found to be "shepherding" satellites, helping to herd the particles that form one of the rings, the so-called epsilon ring. There may be other ring-shepherding satellites orbiting Uranus, but they would have to be smaller than twenty kilometers in diameter, or *Voyager* would have found them.

The single brief visit to the planet Uranus was one of the most informative and exciting episodes in the history of space exploration. The *Voyager* spacecraft performed marvelously, bringing a distant part of our Solar System to life for us, in color and detail that will amaze us for many years to come. The final objects of exploration still lay ahead for it, however, in even farther reaches of space: the planet Neptune and its moons, which you will read about in the next chapter.

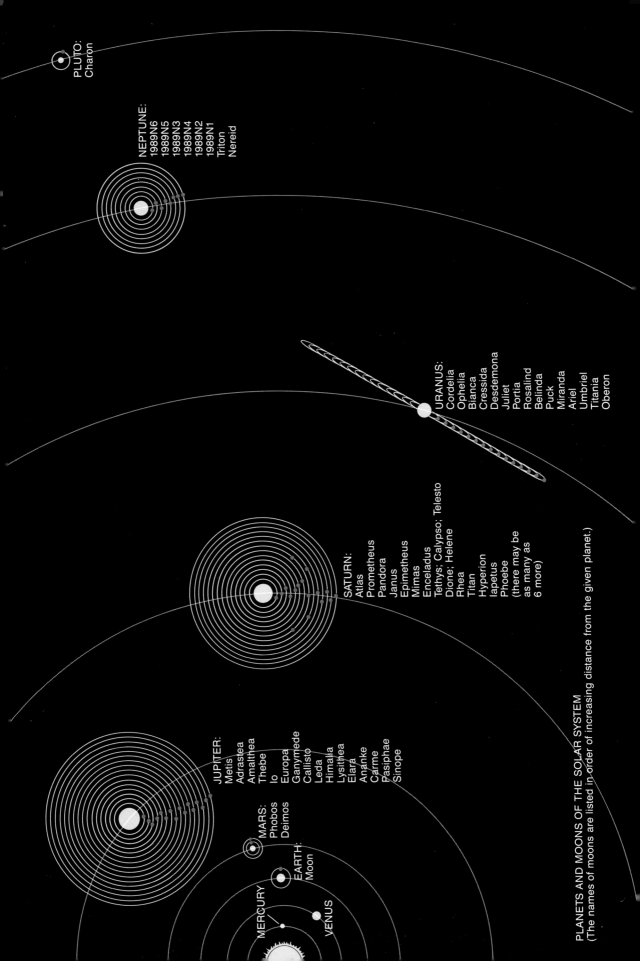

PLUTO:
Charon

NEPTUNE:
1989N6
1989N5
1989N3
1989N4
1989N2
1989N1
Triton
Nereid

URANUS:
Cordelia
Ophelia
Bianca
Cressida
Desdemona
Juliet
Portia
Rosalind
Belinda
Puck
Miranda
Ariel
Umbriel
Titania
Oberon

SATURN:
Atlas
Prometheus
Pandora
Janus
Epimetheus
Mimas
Enceladus
Tethys; Calypso; Telesto
Dione; Helene
Rhea
Titan
Hyperion
Iapetus
Phoebe
(there may be
as many as
6 more)

JUPITER:
Metis
Adrastea
Amalthea
Thebe
Io
Europa
Ganymede
Callisto
Leda
Himalia
Lysithea
Elara
Ananke
Carme
Pasiphae
Sinope

MARS:
Phobos
Deimos

EARTH:
Moon

MERCURY

VENUS

PLANETS AND MOONS OF THE SOLAR SYSTEM
(The names of moons are listed in order of increasing distance from the given planet.)

COLOR PHOTO 1 *Astronauts of Apollo 15 prepare to take their lunar rover on a drive across the dusty surface of Earth's Moon.*

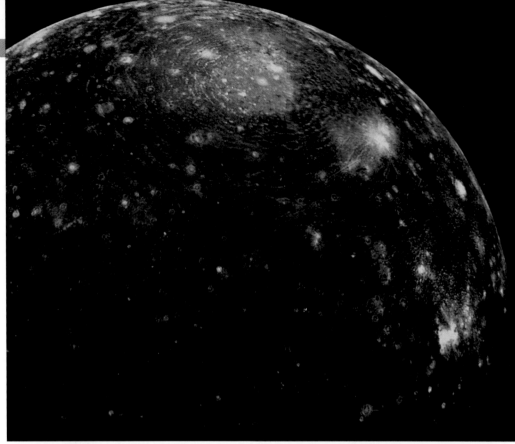

COLOR PHOTO 2 *The battered surface of Callisto. Bright spots are more recent impact areas, in which fresh ice has been exposed.*

COLOR PHOTO 3 *In this close-up of Ganymede, splashes of bright ice are seen among craters, grooves, and dark plains.*

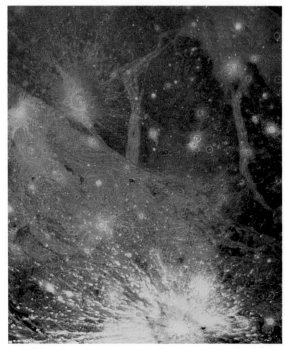

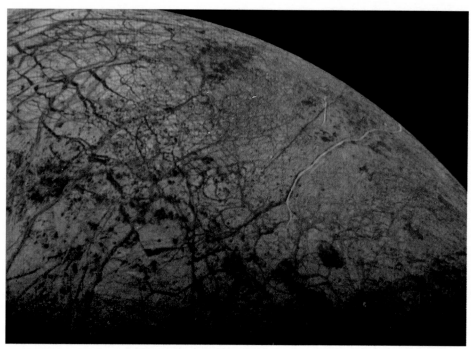

COLOR PHOTO 4 *Close-up of the surface of Europa. There is no evidence in the system of cracks that any of the surface pieces have moved. This suggests that the ice is deep and firm.*

COLOR PHOTO 5 *This amazing image shows Io framed against the colorful clouds of Jupiter.*

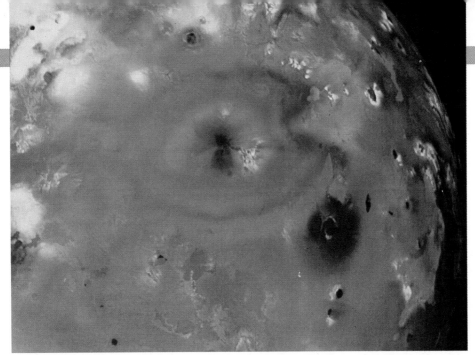

COLOR PHOTO 6 *The dark spot in the center of this picture is an active erupting volcano on Io. The larger dark spot nearby may be a lake of frozen sulfur.*

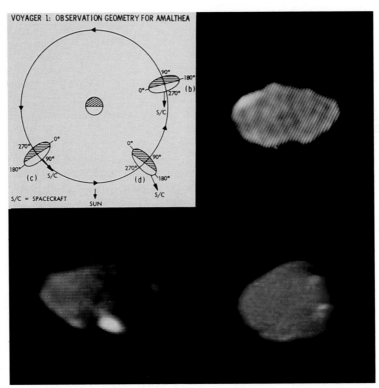

COLOR PHOTO 7 *Three views of Amalthea reveal its potatolike shape and reddish color. The red material may have come from the volcanoes of Io.*

COLOR PHOTO 8 *Iapetus, one of the strangest moons of Saturn. One side is very bright, the other very dark.*

COLOR PHOTO 9 *This high-resolution image of Saturn's moon Dione reveals a great number of craters, including some rather large ones. Dione and many of Saturn's moons are made up mostly of ice.*

COLOR PHOTO 10 *Saturn's moon Tethys is made up mostly of ice and is heavily cratered. Though somewhat similar in appearance to our Moon, it has less than one-third the diameter.*

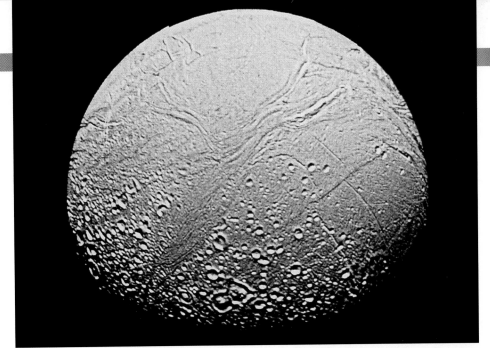

COLOR PHOTO 11 *This is Enceladus, a moon that has one of the brightest surfaces in the Solar System. From this image, you can see some craters and some areas covered with groove patterns similar to those found on Jupiter's moon Ganymede.*

COLOR PHOTO 12 *The large crater of Mimas, seen clearly in this picture, is about 100 kilometers across, about one-quarter of the diameter of this moon.*

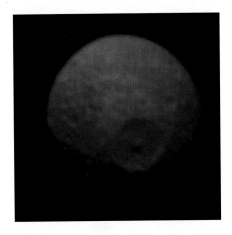

COLOR PHOTO 13 *This image was put together by NASA to show what it might look like to be on Miranda and look toward Uranus.*

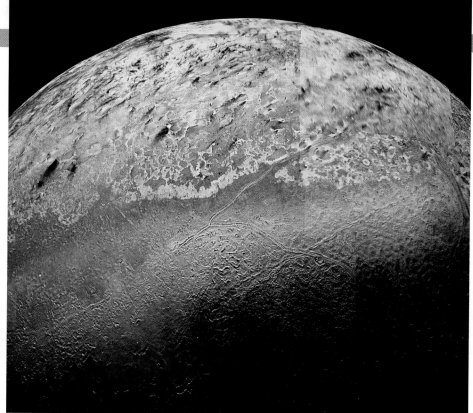

COLOR PHOTO 14 *This image of Neptune's moon Triton is a mosaic made up of many pictures put together. The area at the bottom is the south polar cap. Toward the middle is a bright area covered with frost. The top of the picture shows the northern part of the moon, which was in darkness when* Voyager 2 *flew by.*

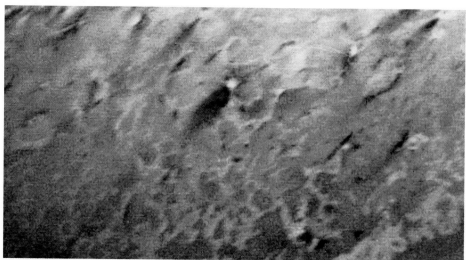

COLOR PHOTO 15 *This image of part of Triton's south polar cap shows some dark streaks that may be the result of geysers. Expanding gaseous and liquid nitrogen may sometimes erupt from these geysers.*

7

NEPTUNE: HIJACKER OF MOONS

Soon after Uranus was discovered by William Herschel in 1781, scientists found that this planet did not orbit the sun in the way they would have predicted. As the decades of its eighty-four-year revolution passed, Uranus was seen to speed up and slow down for no known reason. Astronomers soon guessed that gravity from something, probably another planet, was affecting the orbit of Uranus. Mathematical predictions were made as to the location of this unknown body, and, on September 23, 1846, the planet Neptune was discovered by German astronomer Johann Gottfried Galle.

In August of 1989, Neptune's gravity attracted something else: the *Voyager 2* spacecraft. This, in turn, "attracted" the attention of the world as fantastic new information was sent across a distance of 4.5 billion kilometers to Earth. Once again, spectacular pictures of a distant planet and its rings and moons dazzled both scientists and the general public.

Before the arrival of *Voyager 2*, our knowledge of Neptune and its moons was very sketchy. Through Earth-based telescopes, the planet appeared as a tiny, featureless blue-green disk. On October 10, 1846, very soon after the discovery of Neptune, William Lassell discovered a moon, which was given the name *Triton*. The estimate of its size was arrived at through little more than guesswork, though some thought it might be the largest moon in the Solar System. It was not until May 1, 1949, that a second moon, very small and dim, was discovered. Its discoverer, Gerard P. Kuiper, gave it the name *Nereid*.

Astronomers quickly realized that these two moons were unusual. Triton orbited the planet in the direction opposite the rotation of Neptune, in what is called a retrograde orbit. The only other moons in the Solar System that orbit in this way are the four most distant moons of Jupiter, which are all very small. Triton orbits Neptune at an average distance of about 354,000 kilometers. It takes just over 5 days and 21 hours to complete one revolution.

Nereid also has a strange orbit. Though it is not retrograde, the orbit is tilted more than 27 degrees relative to the equator of Neptune. Even more unusual, the orbit, unlike those of most other moons, is very elliptical, instead of nearly circular. In fact, Nereid can be as close to Neptune as 1.4 million kilometers, or as far away as 9.7 million kilometers. It revolves around the planet in roughly 365 days, almost exactly the length of one Earth year.

Improvements in telescopes failed to provide much more information about Neptune and its moons. Determining the size of Triton was one thing astronomers were able to work at. By making a reasonable guess as to how bright the surface was, they could figure out roughly how large Triton would have to be to reflect the amount of light seen here on Earth. The dimmer the surface was, the larger Triton would have to be to reflect the amount of light it does.

Such an estimate was made assuming a rather unreflective surface. However, the estimate was called into question by infrared-light studies carried out in 1978 by Dale P. Cruikshank. These studies revealed the presence of an atmosphere that contained methane. It was likely that some methane would be frozen on the surface, especially near the poles. Because methane ice is very bright, astronomers began to think parts of

Triton's surface might be highly reflective, which would mean that the moon would have to be somewhat smaller than had been estimated.

Once it became known that all the other large outer planets had rings of rock and ice debris around them, it made sense to look for signs of rings around Neptune. By watching closely as Neptune passed in front of stars, astronomers could see whether the stars would seem to wink on and off as rings intercepted their light. Many astronomers reported observing just this kind of event, but their findings suggested that Neptune might not have a set of complete rings but instead partial rings, or what are called ring arcs. Something better than Earth-based telescopes would be needed to solve the mystery. Astronomers waited for *Voyager 2* to arrive at Neptune and provide answers to their questions.

NEPTUNE: STORMS, BLUE SKIES, AND MOONS

By January of 1989, *Voyager 2* began to reveal Neptunian cloud details in what turned out to be a beautiful blue atmosphere. As the weeks and months passed, more and more detail became visible. Large dark and bright spots—probably resulting from giant storms—could be seen. One of the dark spots turned out to be so big that the entire planet Earth could fit upon it.

It was also discovered that Neptune has a magnetic field. Its magnetic poles are tilted 50 degrees from the rotational poles. Even stranger, a line between the magnetic poles does not pass through or even very near the center of the planet, but is offset from it by almost 10,000 kilometers. Since magnetic fields are thought to be formed by the rotation of a planet's central iron core, it is hard to imagine how this sort of displaced magnetic field could have arisen on Neptune.

The temperature at the cloud tops of Neptune was found to be about –210 degrees Celsius. This is nearly the same as the temperature at the cloud tops of Uranus. Since Neptune receives much less light from the sun than does Uranus, some of the heat that keeps the outer planet's temperature from falling lower must come from inside the planet.

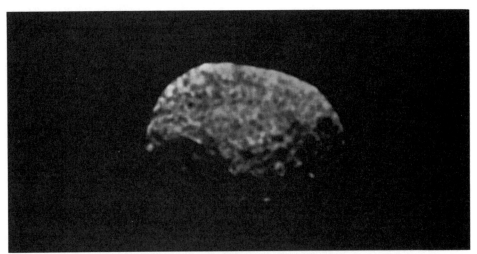

FIGURE 7-1 *This is the most detailed image of 1989N1. Voyager 2 was just 146,000 kilometers away when it took this picture. We now know that 1989N1 is the second-largest moon in the Neptune system, and is about 400 kilometers across.*

The Inner Moons: More Ring Shepherds?

Suddenly, in July, 1989, a point of light was noticed near Neptune. It turned out to be a new moon, which was given the temporary designation 1989N1. (See Figure 7-1.) This moon orbits only 93,000 kilometers above the clouds. When its orbit was calculated, astronomers realized that, just before its closest encounter with Neptune, *Voyager* would pass 1989N1 at a distance of 140,000 kilometers. From that relatively short distance, details as small as three kilometers would be visible.

A few weeks later, three additional moons were found: 1989N2 (See Figure 7-2), 1989N3, and 1989N4. They all orbit even closer to the planet than does 1989N1. All of them are small, probably under 200 kilometers across. Because of glare from the planet Neptune, they can never be seen from Earth.

In addition to aiding in the search for new moons, *Voyager* was also used to look for signs of rings or ring arcs. Two weeks before its closest approach to the planet, a pair of faint strands became visible. One just outside the orbit of 1989N4 appeared to stretch one eighth of the way around Neptune. The second, just 10 degrees (1/36 of a circle) in length, was observed near the orbit of 1989N3.

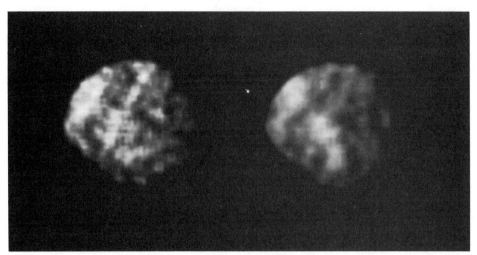

FIGURE 7-2 *Two images of 1989N2 show a small rocky world roughly 200 kilometers across. This Neptunian moon is extremely dark, reflecting only about 5 percent of the light that reaches its surface.*

Four days before its closest approach, *Voyager* began to reveal some of the surface features of Triton, including some areas of strange reddish coloring. Triton turned out to be even brighter than expected, and thus smaller than had been guessed earlier. Two more moons, 1989N5 and 1989N6, also became visible. (See Figure 7-3.) This brought the total number of moons in the Neptune system to eight. Despite some expectations, no other moons would be discovered in the days to come.

One day before encounter, a new computer program was transmitted from Earth, with all the commands needed to continue exploring Neptune and its moons. Further studies of the rings showed that they are not partial arcs, but complete circles. (See Figure 7-4.) At least three of these rings were visible, along with a faint sheet of additional material extending from the innermost ring out to a distance roughly halfway between the outer two rings.

Like some of the small moons of Saturn and Uranus, the inner small moons of Neptune seem to play a role in shepherding the ring particles. Although the rings are complete, they are not uniform. Some regions are thicker than others. This may also be related to the presence of the moons, although a complete explanation does not yet exist.

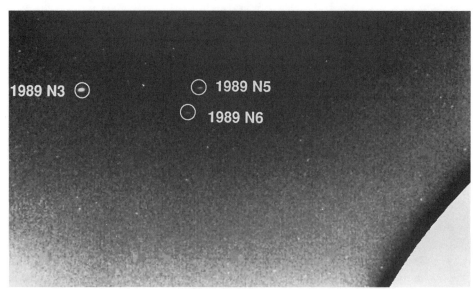

FIGURE 7-3 *The last two moons discovered by* Voyager 2: *1989N5 and 1989N6. They are very small, less than 100 kilometers across, and extremely dark. Their discovery brings the total number of known moons in the Solar System to sixty.*

FIGURE 7-4 *This long-exposure image reveals the ring system of Neptune. The planet has been blocked out so that the faint rings would be visible. You can easily see the three rings that completely surround the planet. You can also make out the faint sheet of material near the rings.*

Nereid: Small and Bright

A picture of the moon Nereid was taken from a distance of 4.7 million kilometers. (See Figure 7-5.) Nereid turned out to be only about 340 kilometers across, smaller than 1989N1, which was revealed in close-up to be about 400 kilometers across. However, Nereid reflects about twice as much light as does 1989N1, since the former moon is composed of lighter-colored material. 1989N1 and the other newly discovered moons turn out to be only about as bright as coal.

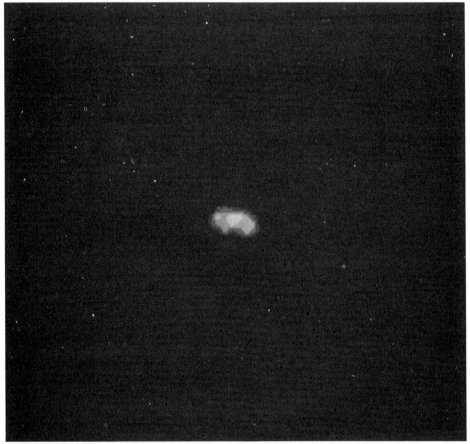

FIGURE 7-5 *This is the best image taken of Nereid, the only Neptunian moon besides Triton known about before* Voyager 2. *The photograph was taken from a distance of 4.7 million kilometers. Nereid is only 340 kilometers across, less than half the size of the newly discovered 1989N1, but it reflects twice as much light. There may be ice on the surface of Nereid.*

TRITON: A MOST INTERESTING WORLD

The Approach to Triton

Less than an hour before its closest encounter, *Voyager* passed undamaged through the ring plane on its way toward Triton and approached Neptune over the planet's north polar region. By the time of closest approach, the gravity of Neptune increased the probe's speed to more than 98,000 kilometers per hour. Six minutes after this approach, *Voyager* passed behind the planet, out of direct contact with Earth. However, the probe continued to send radio signals, using the atmosphere of Neptune to bend, or refract, the signals toward Earth. This technique worked wonderfully, giving scientists more information about the structure of the atmosphere of Neptune and about the gases that make it up. About an hour later, *Voyager* moved out from behind the planet and successfully crossed the ring plane again.

The journey over the north pole of Neptune was designed to bend *Voyager*'s flight path so that it would come as close as possible to Triton. Some scientists already expected this moon to be the most interesting small world visited by *Voyager* during its twelve years in space. They were not to be disappointed.

A little more than two hours after the crossing of the ring plane, the mapping of Triton was begun. Though the moon's surface was still about 200,000 kilometers away, the resulting images would be combined with more-detailed pictures to get the best possible idea about this moon and its formation.

The overall surface of Triton turned out to be amazingly bright, the ice landscape reflecting more than 70 percent of the light that falls upon it. Since so much light energy is reflected, there is little to heat the surface. The temperature on Triton is lower than that of any other place that has been visited in the Solar System, nearly –230 degrees Celsius.

Ice Volcanoes and Geysers

Details of the south polar cap of Triton began to reveal themselves. The cap is very bright, with a hint of red color and some darker streaks. At close range, more than four hours after passing Neptune, *Voyager* revealed

Triton to be an incredible world. Great fields of methane and nitrogen ice cover the south pole and release these substances in gas form into the thin atmosphere. To the north of the cap, approaching the border between day and night on the moon, *Voyager* revealed a region of frost where lower temperatures had reclaimed some of the gases. (See Color Photo 14.)

Beyond the frost region, a vast northern landscape that looks much like the ribbed skin of a cantaloupe was revealed. (See Figure 7-6.) Great cracks

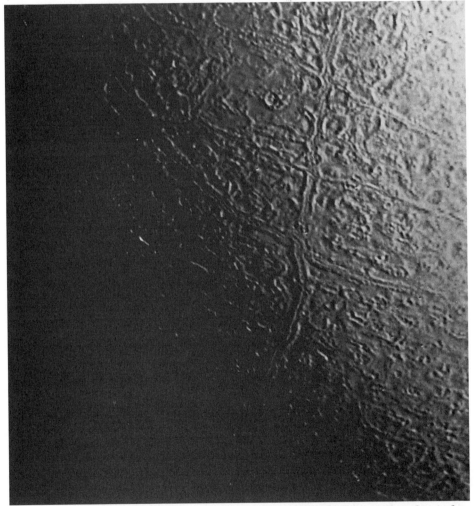

FIGURE 7-6 *The cantaloupe-like surface that is characteristic of much of the northern hemisphere of Triton. Astronomers do not know what forces shaped this strange landscape.*

that are 30 kilometers wide and filled with ice that probably rose from beneath the surface were seen. Also visible were the large vents of flat ice volcanoes surrounded by flooded plains of icy lava that look like giant skating rinks. The volcanoes are not erupting at present. They must have done so in the recent past, however, since few craters are visible on the freshly recoated surface, which is probably one of the youngest in the Solar System. More eruptions may well take place in the future. (See Figure 7-7.)

The dark streaks seen in Triton's southern polar cap may result from geysers. (See Color Photo 15.) Nitrogen trapped far beneath the surface may begin to melt and vaporize during Triton's summer. Expanding as it does so, the nitrogen would push rapidly toward and through the surface, erupting at speeds of 250 meters per second. The liquid and gaseous nitrogen would then crystallize and fall back toward the surface.

Pure nitrogen ice is white, however, and Triton's streaks are dark. The dark color may result from darkened surface methane pulled up during the eruption. The methane ice may have been darkened as a result of being struck by radiation from the sun and by radiation pulled in by the magnetic field of Neptune. This darkened methane ice would produce the streaks as it settled back to the surface of Triton after being thrown up by the geysers. This geyser theory, although it provides the best explanation for the observed features, is not supported by direct evidence from *Voyager 2*, none of whose photos revealed actual eruptions in process.

As *Voyager* continued past Triton, it was made to film a star moving behind this moon. The star seemed to dim as its light passed through Triton's atmosphere, and finally it disappeared behind the moon. Study of these observations revealed that the methane and nitrogen atmosphere of Triton is extremely thin—in fact 100,000 times *thinner* than the atmosphere of Earth.

Triton's Beginnings

Triton's origin has been a mystery for some time. Astronomers now think that Triton may not have begun its existence as a moon of Neptune. It may have actually been another small planet that was orbiting the sun and that got too close to Neptune. It may have been attracted by Neptune's gravity and come close enough to collide with a large Neptunian moon. This collision would have taken away some of Triton's orbital energy, and Neptune would have then captured Triton, pulling it into orbit. The direction from which Triton approached Neptune resulted in the moon's retrograde orbital motion.

At first, Triton probably had a very "stretched out," or elliptical, orbit. The part of the orbit inside Neptune's magnetic field was swept by particles trapped there that slowed down Triton. This energy loss repeatedly kept the moon from moving back as far away from the planet as it had been

FIGURE 7-7 *This close-up of Triton shows what appears to be a large ice volcano, about 200 kilometers across. One fresh crater formed by meteor impact is visible on the floor of the volcano, which, unlike volcanoes on Earth, is actually flat instead of mountainous.*

in preceding revolutions. Gradually, the orbit of Triton became more and more circular. As this process was taking place, tidal forces from the pull of Neptune's gravity melted the interior of Triton, resulting in the volcanic activity that produced much of the landscape observed by *Voyager 2*. Now Triton, as it orbits, keeps the same face toward Neptune, and its orbit is very nearly circular, so there is little tidal force acting on it nowadays. That is why the volcanic activity seems to have slowed or even stopped.

What happened to the moon with which Triton collided? It may have been destroyed, perhaps producing the material that forms the rings and small inner moons of Neptune. Perhaps it collided with Nereid, which would help to explain the highly elliptical orbit of that moon. It is difficult to say for certain. We do know that whatever happened must have taken place about four billion years ago.

We hope to be able to gain a better understanding of the future of Triton. Because it revolves around Neptune in retrograde fashion, energy is being lost from its orbit. The moon will slowly fall closer toward Neptune, and sometime in the future will either be ripped apart by tidal forces or will fall into the planet. Most estimates today are that these things will not happen for at least 100 million years.

The visit to Neptune and its moons was in many ways the landmark of the *Voyager* missions. Scientists made use of an alignment of the outer planets that occurs only once every 177 years and that made possible *Voyager 2*'s visit to Neptune, after it had visited Jupiter, Saturn, and Uranus. It will thus be a long time before we pass that way a second time. What we learned from *Voyager 2* must serve as the basis for our knowledge of Neptune and its moons for many decades to come.

Voyager 2 will continue on, still sending information back to Earth. Along with *Voyager 1* and the earlier *Pioneer 10* and *Pioneer 11* spacecraft, it will head out of the Solar System. All these probes will be searching for what is called the heliopause. That is the edge of the sun's area of direct nongravitational influence in space, the farthest extent of the solar wind. The electrical power system on the *Voyager* spacecraft should continue to function until about the year 2020. Then it will go silent and coast, unpowered, to the stars.

PLUTO: THE ROAD NEVER TRAVELED

Only one planet in our Solar System remains unvisited. The *Voyager* spacecraft are now traveling away from the Solar System, one above and the other below the plane of the planets, and will not be able to explore Pluto. To reach Pluto with a spacecraft like *Voyager* without using a gravity assist from Jupiter or Saturn would take about fifty years. Since neither of those major planets is in a favorable position relative to Pluto, it is safe to say that Pluto will remain unvisited for quite a few years to come.

THE ODDITIES OF PLUTO

In some ways, you might think that we are not missing much in failing to explore Pluto. It is, after all, a very small planet, probably just over half the diameter of our Moon. Astronomers, however, are very interested in

Pluto. It probably has a history unlike that of any of the other planets. In fact, it may be more like Neptune's moon Triton than it is like any other planet.

Pluto was discovered in 1930 by astronomer Clyde Tombaugh. The existence of Pluto had been predicted by other astronomers to help explain some strangeness of motion in the orbit of Neptune. They had expected Pluto to be a rather large planet, at least twice the mass of Earth. Only in the last few decades have we come to realize that Pluto is actually the smallest planet in the Solar System.

Pluto travels in a very strange orbit, one that is not in the same plane as the other planets. The orbit is tilted, or inclined, by 17 degrees. The orbit is also unusually elliptical. It is, in fact, so stretched out that Pluto can be anywhere between 4.5 billion and 7.4 billion kilometers from the sun. Sometimes, Pluto is actually inside the orbit of Neptune. In fact, since 1979, it has been a bit closer to the sun than is Neptune, and will remain so until 1999. This 20-year period is only a fraction of Pluto's 248-year orbit. During the rest of the time, Pluto is the planet farthest from the sun.

CHARON: FERRYMAN OF THE UNDERWORLD

Pluto's strange orbit seems more like that of an asteroid than a planet, and asteroidlike bodies do not usually have moons. Therefore, no one really expected to find a moon around Pluto. However, in July of 1978, a striking image of Pluto was obtained by a large telescope owned by the U.S. Naval Observatory. In this image, Pluto appeared to have a bump! Further study identified this bump as a moon a little less than half the diameter of Pluto. (See Figure 8-1.) The moon was named Charon, after the mythological ferryman who carried souls across the river Styx to the god Pluto's kingdom of the dead, called Hades. The Styx was one of the five rivers that separated Hades from the land of the living.

Although both the "underworld" planet and its moon are small, Charon is still large relative to Pluto. In fact, no other planet–moon pair are nearly this close to each other in size. For this reason, some astronomers refer to Pluto and Charon together as a double planet.

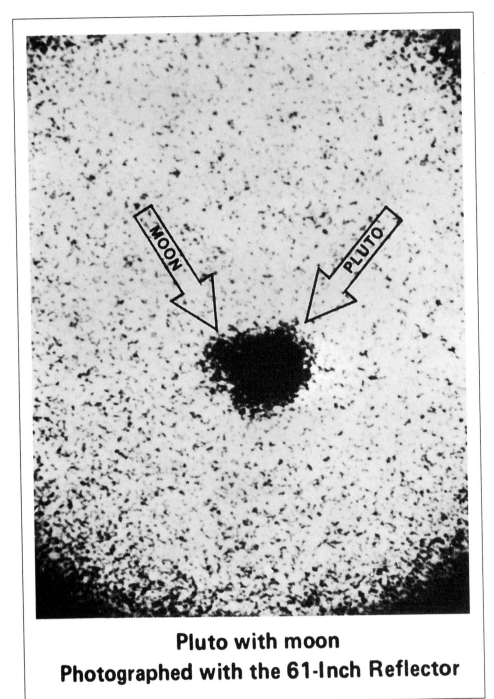

**Pluto with moon
Photographed with the 61-Inch Reflector**

FIGURE 8-1 *This image was the first to indicate the existence of Pluto's moon, Charon.*

THE ORIGINS OF PLUTO AND CHARON

It was once thought that Pluto was an escaped moon of Neptune. Although Pluto does pass inside the orbit of Neptune, it is several hundred million kilometers north of Neptune when the orbits cross, so it seems unlikely to have started out as a Neptunian moon. Besides, as we now know, it has a moon of its own.

Other astronomers have suggested that Pluto is made up of the remains of a giant comet. The comet may have originally moved in an orbit that extended far beyond any of the planets. It may have collided with a large object, losing much of its orbital energy in the process. Slowed down in this way, it could then have been captured into its present orbit around the sun. The moon Charon may be what is left of the object that collided with the comet that became Pluto.

There is a more likely explanation, however. Pluto may be what is called a planetesimal. Thousands or even millions of such bodies formed from the collapsing cloud of gas and dust that formed the Solar System five billion years ago. Many of these bodies collided with each other and became bound together by gravity, in a process called *accretion,* to form the planets. Pluto may have simply failed to take sufficient part in accretion to have become a larger planet, but instead captured one smaller planetesimal that became the moon Charon.

ECLIPSES THAT REVEAL ALL

Normally, it would be very hard, if not impossible, to learn much about Pluto and Charon. They are both so far away and so small that they appear as little more than fuzzy dots through our most powerful telescopes. The orbital period of Charon, about 6.4 days, was soon determined, however, as was the distance between Pluto and Charon, which is about 19,300 kilometers. Their exact sizes remained a mystery for some time, and, until recently, there were few clues as to what their surfaces are like.

A fortunate thing has happened, however: Pluto and Charon have begun a process in which they eclipse one another. This sort of event happens only once every 124 years, half the orbital period of Pluto. During these times, Charon passes directly in front of Pluto, blocking the sun's light, and then passes directly behind the planet. Because Pluto moves so slowly in its orbit, each series of eclipses lasts several years. Just this sort of eclipse "season" began in 1985, and will last until 1991. By studying what happens to the light reflected from Pluto and Charon during these eclipses, astronomers will be able to discover a great deal about these worlds.

The eclipse has already allowed determination of the diameters of Pluto and Charon. Astronomers at the University of Hawaii have found Pluto to be only 2,290 kilometers across, and Charon 1,285 kilometers across. These figures are quite a bit lower than earlier estimates and indicate that the two bodies are denser and rockier than had been expected.

The amount of light coming from Pluto and Charon changes during the eclipse cycle, and this has helped scientists find out how bright the surfaces of these worlds are. Pluto reflects about 60 percent of the sunlight reaching its surface, and Charon reflects about 40 percent. This indicates a difference between their surfaces.

Since Charon is darker, it is now assumed to absorb more heat from the sun and should be a bit warmer than Pluto. "Warm" this far from the sun, however, is nothing like warm here on Earth. The temperatures at the surface of Pluto and Charon are generally somewhere around −220 degrees Celsius. The two bodies may be a bit warmer than that now, since Pluto is in that part of its orbit nearest the sun.

Studies of light from Pluto have indicated the existence of an atmosphere around that planet. The atmosphere is probably quite thin and is composed of methane and traces of other gases. There is probably methane ice on the surface as well. This gives the surface a reddish color. Pluto may in fact look quite a bit like Neptune's moon Triton.

Charon is so small that any atmosphere it may have is extremely thin. One of the reasons Charon does not reflect as much sunlight could be that there is less methane ice on its surface. Its higher temperature and lower gravity, relative to Pluto, would allow more of its methane to escape as a gas. Instead of much methane, there appears to be a gray frost of water ice on Charon.

AN IMAGINARY VISIT TO CHARON

Imagine, if you will, the view you would have if you were standing on the surface of Charon today. A crescent Pluto would hang low in the sky but would not seem to move, since Charon always keeps the same face toward Pluto (just as our Moon always keeps the same face toward Earth). This crescent shape would point toward the very distant sun, which would be just a bright point of light in the dark sky. A faint reddish glow above the crescent would reveal Pluto's thin, cold atmosphere. The landscape of Charon around you would be dark, with scattered patches of frost twinkling dimly among the rocks and hills. You would have to keep your spacesuit heater turned up while you made these observations, for it is so cold on Charon that your flesh would instantly crystallize if it were exposed to the severe environment. Yet, it is now summer on Charon! In the years to come, Pluto and Charon will move farther from the sun and become even colder, and Pluto's thin atmosphere will begin to condense and freeze on the surface.

We cannot in reality visit Charon or Pluto any time soon. As we continue our examination of the nearer planets of the Solar System, the mysteries of Pluto and Charon will continue to lure us outward. We can only hope that, one day, when higher-speed spacecraft that quickly travel great distances can be built, we shall finally turn our eyes directly upon the cold landscapes of the "underworld" planet and its ferryman moon.

JUST A FEW
BILLION MORE
SMALL WORLDS

As you have seen, there are sixty known moons in the Solar System. There may be some others, orbiting Pluto or some as yet undiscovered planet beyond. The moon count does not have to stop with the discovery of already existing moons, however. Someday, we may actually add new moons, here around Earth or around other planets where they would be useful for various purposes. Where would we get these new moons? One of the likeliest sources lies in a region between the orbits of the planets Mars and Jupiter and contains thousands of rocky bodies, ranging in diameter from hundreds of kilometers down to a few centimeters. A second likely source lies for the most part beyond the orbit of the planet Pluto and is the "home base" for other bodies that are made up mostly of water ice.

Exploration missions to these regions will not be carried out for many years. When they are, however, they will usher in a fantastic time for all humanity—a time when there will be plenty of resources made available, enough to serve the needs of all the people likely to live on our planet. As we take a look at these regions and the bodies they contain, you will begin to see how all of this might become possible.

ASTEROIDS

Celestial Missing Links

On the first day of the nineteenth century, January 1, 1801, a type of heavenly body never before observed revealed its existence to human beings. An Italian astronomer, Giuseppe Piazzi, noticed an object in the constellation Taurus that moved among the stars. The rapid motion of the object showed that it must be within the Solar System.

Piazzi became seriously ill soon after he made his discovery and was unable to continue observing the object. Other astronomers began trying to find the mysterious body, suspecting that it might be a new planet. At the end of the year, a great German mathematician, Carl Friedrich Gauss, using the data collected by Piazzi, predicted where the object might be found. It turned out to be exactly where he said it would, some 400 million kilometers from the sun, between the orbits of Mars and Jupiter.

This discovery of an object between these two planetary objects filled a gap in the Solar System that had mystified astronomers for some time. Two eighteenth-century German astronomers, Johann Titius and Johann Bode, had discovered this gap during a study of the relationships between planetary orbits. They had found that each successive planet known in their day has an orbit about 75 percent larger than that of the preceding planet. The only exception involves the planets Mars and Jupiter. There is no planet that has an orbit 75 percent bigger than that of Mars. The newly discovered object turned out to orbit at just about the correct distance to fill in this gap. This was an exciting discovery for the astronomers of that time, especially when it turned out that Jupiter's orbit was about 75 percent larger than that of the object.

It was therefore natural for scientists to assume that the new object discovered in 1801 was a planet. However, the object, which was named Ceres after the mythical Roman goddess of the harvest, had a surprise in store. It turned out to be only about 1,000 kilometers across, which is smaller than any of the other planets and less than one third the size of our Moon. It was in fact the smallest object in outer space known at that time. This led some astronomers to believe that Ceres was not a planet. They continued to search this area of the Solar System for signs of a larger body.

Instead, they found more small ones. By the end of the century, several hundred of them were found. Today, we know of more than three thousand. Astronomers think there may be over twenty thousand of these objects, which are called asteroids. The four discovered earliest—Ceres and three others, named Pallas, Vesta, and Juno—travel in orbits in the gap between Mars and Jupiter. Hundreds of smaller ones also orbit there. This region is now known as the main belt of asteroids, because it contains so many of these bodies.

Some of the asteroids not found in the main belt cross planetary orbits. The so-called Apollo objects are asteroids that cross the orbit of the earth, occasionally coming as close to our planet as a few million kilometers. Amor objects are asteroids that cross the orbit of Mars. There are other asteroids, called Trojans, that travel in the orbit of Jupiter 60 degrees ahead of or behind the planet. Many of these are likely to have originated in the main belt.

Unusual Worlds with Unusual Beginnings

The four asteroids Ceres, Pallas, Vesta, and Juno are the easiest to study, as they are large and bright enough to be seen through small telescopes. Ceres is by far the largest of these. Its mass is about 30 percent of the total estimated mass of all the asteroids combined. Unlike many of the others, it is not irregular in shape, but nearly spherical. It is quite dark in color, reflecting only about 4 percent of the sunlight reaching its surface. The asteroids Pallas and Vesta are each about 500 kilometers across, and Juno is only 250. Pallas is about as dark as Ceres, whereas Juno is about twice as bright. Vesta is among the brightest of the asteroids, reflecting back into space about 20 percent of the sunlight that reaches its surface.

It was once thought that these and the other asteroids in the main belt were created by a collision, either between two planets that once orbited between Mars and Jupiter, or between a single planet in that region and a wandering object. The collision was thought to have resulted in a shattering that produced many smaller fragments.

The presence of nearby Jupiter, however, is now thought to make this earlier theory unlikely. The gravitational pull of this giant planet has always been so strong that it would have disturbed any normal process of planet formation near it. It seems unlikely, therefore, that any planet was ever able to form near it, in the main-belt region. It is probable that, instead, fragments that were originally present collected and merged to form many asteroids. Numerous actual collisions and near misses further broke these asteroids into smaller ones and scattered some of them into other regions of the Solar System.

Asteroids with Moons

The irregular shape observed in many asteroids can be explained on the basis of collisions with other objects. Some of the most recent studies indicate, however, that the elongated shape apparently observed in a few asteroids may be due to the presence of pairs of objects once thought to be single asteroids. These binary asteroids are made up of two separate bodies that orbit each other. One binary asteroid, named Hector, seems to be made up of two objects so close to each other that they may in fact occasionally scrape against each other. At least two other asteroids, Pallas and Victoria, appear to have smaller, moonlike asteroids orbiting about them. Asteroids are very interesting objects indeed.

Meteorites: Clues to the Asteroids

Asteroids are of different colors. These colors differ because the materials on the asteroids' surfaces are different. The colors of light, or spectra, reflected back to us from them are being studied to help indicate when and how the asteroids were formed.

Astronomers are also learning more about asteroids by studying the composition of meteorites collected here on Earth. Meteorites are the remains of meteors, also known as shooting stars, that survive their fiery descent through our atmosphere. There seem to be many similarities between the compositions of asteroids and meteorites. In fact, it has long been thought by many astronomers that many meteorites came from asteroids.

Meteorites seem to be of two basic types, in terms of the material that makes them up. Those of one type are dense and are rich in iron. Those of the other type are made up of a mixture of lightweight rocky materials.

Meteorites of the two types probably came from different parts of single larger asteroids formed out of the cloud of dust and gas from which the Solar System formed. As the material in these asteroids collected, temperatures rose. The rock melted, and the heavier, iron-rich materials sank toward the core while the lighter, rocky material rose. Once the asteroids cooled, impacts with other objects at first broke away the outer layers of rocky crust, forming rocky objects, some of which eventually became rocky meteorites. Some of the remaining iron-rich asteroid cores eventually became iron-rich meteorites.

Study of meteorites has suggested that the variance in color and surface composition of different asteroids is due to the differing relative amounts of rocky and iron-rich materials at their surfaces. The ratio in any given asteroid is now assumed to depend upon the degree of heating that occurred when the asteroid formed. The hotter an asteroid eventually became, the more separation was possible between materials. In very hot asteroids, the molten state of the cores allowed the heavier metallic material to sink in, causing more of the less-dense rocky material to be pushed out to the surface.

The Mother Lode of Space

The metal content of asteroids is what makes them so important to our future. The idea of actually mining asteroids for the valuable metal ores they contain has been under consideration for some time now. In "Pioneering the Space Frontier," a report of the National Commission on Space, it was suggested that the amount of recoverable material in the main asteroid belt may be enough to support a population thousands of times larger than that of Earth today. It is exciting to think that so many resources may eventually be within our reach.

From a base on Mars, explorers might one day set out to sample the surfaces of asteroids, looking for those that could quickly be made to produce valuable material. Mining teams would then set out for short stays at the locations that offer the best prospects. Giant vehicles called mass drivers would be used to push these asteroids into new orbits that would bring them closer to wherever their wealth of resources would be needed.

Though small compared to planets and most moons, the asteroids may then turn out to be among the most useful of small worlds in our Solar System. They may greatly improve our prospects for future exploration and colonization of space. Without them, acquiring necessary material would be much more expensive and difficult. Lifting these resources from the surface of our planet, the Moon, or any other major body of the inner Solar System instead and moving them to the desired sites in distant space would require the use of much more fuel and pose many more problems. The first major step toward the eventual goal of using asteroids for these purposes will most likely be made sometime during the 1990s, when the first unmanned space probe will probably visit an asteroid.

COMETS

The Most Abundant of Small Worlds

Asteroids number only in the thousands, but other nonplanetary small worlds, called comets, probably number in the billions. Comets are like giant icebergs in space. They may be as much as several miles across—rather small compared to most moons or asteroids. Because they are also very far away most of the time, they are usually very difficult to see. Only a few comets per century appear as visible objects, and then only for a few weeks or months. (See Figure 9-1.) They spend much of the rest of their time in the frozen depths of the outer Solar System, in a huge spherical region far outside the orbit of Pluto, known as the Oort cloud. Most comets—and all of them that come close to Earth—move in highly eccentric elliptical orbits. They develop long "tails" as a result of the streaming of material that is pushed outward by particles and radiation called the solar wind. A comet's tail always points away from the sun, even when the comet is moving away from it.

By far the most famous comet is Halley's comet, which visited the inner Solar System in late 1985 and early 1986. At that time, it was visible to the naked eye. The sight of this comet was a once-in-a-lifetime treat for most

FIGURE 9-1 *A photographer for a Melbourne, Australia, newspaper caught a comet passing over the city in 1947.*

FIGURE 9-2 *Halley's comet, outward bound, 106.5 million miles from Earth at a relative speed of 121,000 miles per hour, photographed from Virginia in May, 1986.*

of its viewers, since the comet follows an orbit that returns it to our vicinity only once every seventy-six years. (See Figure 9-2.)

Although Halley's comet was studied and observed from Earth, far more was learned about it by the use of instruments on spacecraft. The governments of Japan, the Soviet Union, and several European countries sent probes to examine this spectacular visitor close up. The probes provided exciting new data. The comet's surface turned out to be much darker than was earlier thought. It has an albedo, or brightness, of only about 0.04, making it among the darkest objects in the Solar System— blacker, in fact, than soot. The comet's head is shaped somewhat like a potato. Below its dusty black crust, there is a great deal of water. In fact, like other comets, it is mostly water. So it indeed makes sense to think of comets as cosmic icebergs.

What to Do with a Comet

The large quantity of water in comets could make them vital to our future in space. Many of the worlds of our Solar System that we may eventually explore and colonize in the next few centuries (such as Mars and our Moon) are very dry. Comets could help to supply all the water we shall ever need on these worlds.

There are a couple of ways the comets could be made to do this. They could be redirected to crash into the surface of the world on which we would hope eventually to settle. This would release clouds of water vapor around that world. Such a project might have some special value on Mars, which already has a thin atmosphere. The additional water vapor would give it a denser atmosphere that would be better able to hold heat from the sun. That could go a long way toward making Mars a more Earthlike planet.

A less violent alternative to the collision method involves directing comets into orbit around the dry worlds of interest. The comets could then be "mined" for their water content, and this precious resource could then easily be dropped to the surfaces of these worlds, by means of reusable cargo vehicles. A single comet mined in this way could provide enough water to supply a large base on any suitable world of the Solar System for many years. (See Figures 9-3a and b.)

FIGURE 9-3a *A five-minute time exposure of Comet MRKOS, taken by a Texas photographer in 1957 as it swept below the bowl of the Big Dipper.*

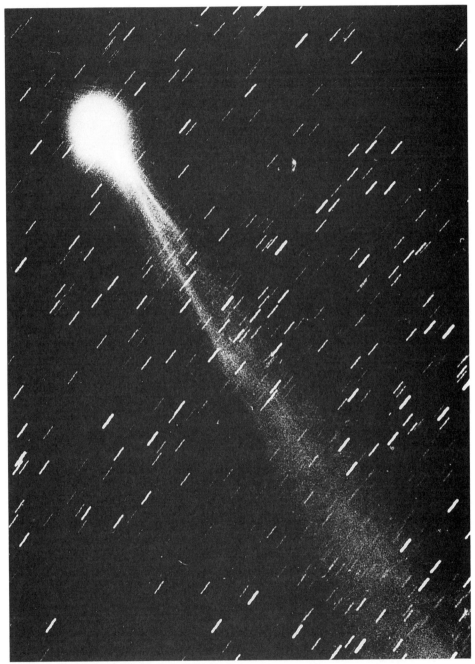

FIGURE 9-3b *Tago-Sato-Kosaka comet, photographed in 1970, 35 million miles from the earth and about 90 million miles from the sun. Its tail, made up of gas and dust filaments, is about 3 million miles long.*

And so, we can expect that by using asteroids and comets we shall one day add to the number of moons orbiting the planets in our Solar System. The process of moon-making will no longer be a random one left to nature. We shall carry it out ourselves to aid us in exploring and colonizing our planetary neighbors.

In the far-distant future, we may even be able to apply this and other methods in the exploration of star systems other than our own. Our Milky Way contains over a hundred billion stars, and many of them have planets, comets, and asteroids orbiting them, and moons orbiting the planets—all of them just waiting to be explored. And the Milky Way is only one of billions of galaxies. The total number of small worlds in our universe is beyond imagining. Judging by what we know about the ones already discovered, each is apt to be fascinating in its own way—small in size but great in terms of wonder and the promise of endless adventure.

A
CHECKLIST
OF MOONS

his checklist contains information on all moons for which an orbit
has been established. The moons are arranged by planet, starting
with the planets nearest to the sun. The moons for each planet
are listed in order of increasing distance from the planet, starting
with those nearest to it. The number of known moons for each planet is noted
in parentheses after the planet's name.

Key to information:
NAME OF PLANET (number of moons)
Name of moon (discoverer, year)
Diameter of moon: kilometers/miles
Average distance from planet: kilometers/miles
Orbital period, or time to orbit planet: days, hours, minutes
Mass of moon, relative to mass of Earth's Moon, which is assigned a value of 1
Gravity at surface, relative to Earth's gravity, which is assigned a value of 1
Eccentricity
Albedo
Visual magnitude
Special characteristics

Eccentricity indicates how elongated an orbit is. It ranges from 0 (for a perfectly circular orbit) to 1 or even higher. A very eccentric orbit often indicates that a moon is a captured asteroid. A more circular orbit indicates that the moon was probably formed at about the time its planet formed.

Albedo indicates the fraction of the light that is reflected from the surface of a moon. It ranges between 0 (for a completely nonreflective moon) and 1 (for a completely reflective moon). Brighter moons are most likely covered with ice. Darker, low-albedo moons are typically rocky.

Visual magnitude is a measure of how bright an astronomical object appears from the surface of the earth. The smaller the number, the brighter is the object. Very bright objects have negative visual magnitudes. The sun, for example, has a visual magnitude of –27. A person with average eyesight can see objects about as dim as a + 6 magnitude. A good pair of binoculars will reveal objects down to about + 8 or + 9. A high-quality six-inch reflecting telescope will reveal objects down to about + 13.5 magnitude. Dimmer objects require larger, and much more expensive, instruments.

Some of the values of quantities such as mass and gravity are listed as *uncertain*. In such cases, the moons are very small. It is safe to assume that their masses and gravities are much smaller than those of our Moon.

Special characteristics are those of particular interest. They are not listed for all moons. Those moons without such notes are generally typical, heavily cratered, rocky worlds.

MERCURY (0)

VENUS (0)

EARTH (1)
The Moon, or Luna (discoverer and date of discovery unknown)
Diameter: 3,476 km/2,160 mi
Distance from Earth: 384,500 km/239,000 mi

Orbital period: 27 days, 7 hours, 44 minutes

Mass: 1 (approx. 73,500,000,000,000,000,000,000,000 kilograms)

Gravity: 0.16

Eccentricity: 0.0549

Albedo: 0.11

Visual magnitude: −12.7

Special characteristics: only world besides Earth on which humans have ever set foot

MARS (2)

Phobos (A. Hall, 1877)

Diameter: 21 km/13 mi

Distance from Mars: 9,400 km/5,850 mi

Orbital period: 7 hours, 40 minutes

Mass: 0.00000018

Gravity: 0.0008

Eccentricity: 0.015

Albedo: 0.07

Visual magnitude: 11.6

Special characteristics: possibly captured asteroid; somewhat potato-shaped; many craters and grooves; probably next world on which humans will set foot

Deimos (A. Hall, 1877)

Diameter: 12 km/7.5 mi

Distance from Mars: 23,500 km/14,600 mi

Orbital period: 1 day, 6 hours, 19 minutes

Mass: 0.00000002

Gravity: 0.0003

Eccentricity: 0.0005

Albedo: 0.07

Visual magnitude: 12.7

Special characteristics: similar to Phobos, but with fine dust covering

JUPITER (16)

Metis (S. Synnott, 1979)

Diameter: 40 km/25 mi

Distance from Jupiter: 128,000 km/79,550 mi

Orbital period: 7 hours, 4 minutes

Mass: uncertain

Gravity: uncertain

Eccentricity: 0

Albedo: 0.05

Visual magnitude: 17.5

Special characteristics: orbits just inside the orbit of Jupiter's primary ring

Adrastea (Jewitt, Danielson, Synnott, 1979)

Diameter: 25 km/16 mi

Distance from Jupiter: 129,000 km/80,200 mi

Orbital period: 7 hours, 8 minutes

Mass: uncertain

Gravity: uncertain

Eccentricity: 0

Albedo: 0.05

Visual magnitude: 18.7

Special characteristics: orbits just outside the orbit of Jupiter's primary ring

Amalthea (E. Barnard, 1892)

Diameter: 170 km/105 mi

Distance from Jupiter: 180,000 km/112,000 mi

Orbital period: 11 hours, 57 minutes

Mass: uncertain

Gravity: uncertain

Eccentricity: 0.003

Albedo: 0.05

Visual magnitude: 14.1

Special characteristics: reddish color perhaps due to material from volcanoes of Io; irregular shape

Thebe (S. Synnott, 1979)
Diameter: 100 km/60 mi
Distance from Jupiter: 222,000 km/138,000 mi
Orbital period: 16 hours, 11 minutes
Mass: uncertain
Gravity: uncertain
Eccentricity: 0.013
Albedo: 0.05
Visual magnitude: 16.0
Special characteristics: dark and rocky; perhaps a captured asteroid

Io (G. Galilei, 1610)
Diameter: 3,630 km/2,250 mi
Distance from Jupiter: 422,000 km/262,000 mi
Orbital period: 1 day, 18 hours, 28 minutes
Mass: 1.214
Gravity: 0.188
Eccentricity: 0.004
Albedo: 0.6
Visual magnitude: 5.0
Special characteristics: only world in the Solar System besides Earth known
    to have active volcanoes; spectacular orange and red coloration caused by
    volcanic release of sulfur from beneath the surface

Europa (G. Galilei, 1610)
Diameter: 3,140 km/1,950 mi
Distance from Jupiter: 671,000 km/417,000 mi
Orbital period: 3 days, 13 hours, 13 minutes
Mass: 0.663
Gravity: 0.137
Eccentricity: 0.010
Albedo: 0.6
Visual magnitude: 5.3
Special characteristics: surface entirely ice covered; very few craters; cracks
    covering much of the surface; possibly an ocean beneath the ice

Ganymede (G. Galilei, 1610)
Diameter: 5,260 km/3,270 mi
Distance from Jupiter: 1,070,000 km/665,000 mi
Orbital period: 7 days, 3 hours, 43 minutes
Mass: 2.027
Gravity: 0.15
Eccentricity: 0.001
Albedo: 0.4
Visual magnitude: 4.6
Special characteristics: largest of the known moons of the Solar System;
    various types of surface; some areas heavily cratered, others covered with
    patterns of grooves

Callisto (G. Galilei, 1610)
Diameter: 4,800 km/2,980 mi
Distance from Jupiter: 1,885,000 km/1,170,000 mi
Orbital period: 16 days, 16 hours, 32 minutes
Mass: 1.463
Gravity: 0.13
Eccentricity: 0.007
Albedo: 0.2
Visual magnitude: 5.6
Special characteristics: most heavily cratered object in the Solar System

Leda (C. Kowal, 1974)
Diameter: 15 km/9 mi
Distance from Jupiter: 11,110,000 km/6,900,000 mi
Orbital period: 240 days
Mass: uncertain
Gravity: uncertain
Eccentricity: 0.147
Albedo: uncertain
Visual magnitude: 20
Special characteristics: may have come from the same parent body as Himalia,
    Lysithea, and Elara

Himalia (C. Perrine, 1904)
Diameter: 185 km/115 mi
Distance from Jupiter: 11,470,000 km/7,130,000 mi
Orbital period: 251 days
Mass: uncertain
Gravity: uncertain
Eccentricity: 0.158
Albedo: 0.03
Visual magnitude: 14.8
Special characteristics: may have come from the same parent body as Leda, Lysithea, and Elara

Lysithea (S. Nicholson, 1938)
Diameter: 35 km/22 mi
Distance from Jupiter: 11,710,000 km/7,278,000 mi
Orbital period: 260 days
Mass: uncertain
Gravity: uncertain
Eccentricity: 0.130
Albedo: uncertain
Visual magnitude: 18.4
Special characteristics: may have come from the same parent body as Leda, Himalia, and Elara

Elara (C. Perrine, 1905)
Diameter: 75 km/47 mi
Distance from Jupiter: 11,740,000 km/7,296,000 mi
Orbital period: 260 days
Mass: uncertain
Gravity: uncertain
Eccentricity: 0.207
Albedo: 0.03
Visual magnitude: 16.8
Special characteristics: may have come from the same parent body as Leda, Himalia, and Lysithea

Ananke (S. Nicholson, 1951)

Diameter: 30 km/19 mi

Distance from Jupiter: 20,700,000 km/12,865,000 mi

Orbital period: 617 days

Mass: uncertain

Gravity: uncertain

Eccentricity: 0.17

Albedo: uncertain

Visual magnitude: 18.9

Special characteristics: may have come from the same parent body as Carme, Pasiphae, and Sinope

Carme (S. Nicholson, 1938)

Diameter: 40 km/25 mi

Distance from Jupiter: 22,350,000 km/13,890,000 mi

Orbital period: 692 days

Mass: uncertain

Gravity: uncertain

Eccentricity: 0.21

Albedo: uncertain

Visual magnitude: 18.0

Special characteristics: may have come from the same parent body as Ananke, Pasiphae, and Sinope

Pasiphae (P. Melotte, 1908)

Diameter: 50 km/30 mi

Distance from Jupiter: 23,330,000 km/14,500,000 mi

Orbital period: 735 days

Mass: uncertain

Gravity: uncertain

Eccentricity: 0.38

Albedo: uncertain

Visual magnitude: 17.1

Special characteristics: may have come from the same parent body as Ananke, Carme, and Sinope

Sinope (S. Nicholson, 1914)

Diameter: 35 km/22 mi

Distance from Jupiter: 23,370,000 km/14,525,000 mi

Orbital period: 758 days

Mass: uncertain

Gravity: uncertain

Eccentricity: 0.28

Albedo: uncertain

Visual magnitude: 18.3

Special characteristics: may have come from the same parent body as Ananke, Carme, and Pasiphae

SATURN (17) (There may be up to six additional small moons.)

Atlas (R. Terrile, 1980)

Diameter: 30 km/19 mi

Distance from Saturn: 137,000 km/85,000 mi

Orbital period: 14 hours, 25 minutes

Mass: uncertain

Gravity: uncertain

Eccentricity: 0.002

Albedo: 0.4

Visual magnitude: 18.0

Special characteristics: may help shepherd A-ring particles

Prometheus, or 1980S27 (S. Collins, D. Carlson, 1980)

Diameter: 100 km/60 mi

Distance from Saturn: 139,000 km/86,300 mi

Orbital period: 14 hours, 43 minutes

Mass: uncertain

Gravity: uncertain

Eccentricity: 0.004

Albedo: 0.6

Visual magnitude: 15.0

Special characteristics: may help shepherd F-ring particles

Pandora, or 1980S26 (S. Collins, D. Carlson, 1980)
Diameter: 90 km/56 mi
Distance from Saturn: 142,000 km/88,250 mi
Orbital period: 15 hours, 4 minutes
Mass: uncertain
Gravity: uncertain
Eccentricity: 0.004
Albedo: 0.5
Visual magnitude: 16.0
Special characteristics: may help shepherd F-ring particles

Janus (A. Dollfus, 1966)
Diameter: 190 km/120 mi
Distance from Saturn: 151,000 km/94,000 mi
Orbital period: 16 hours, 41 minutes
Mass: uncertain
Gravity: uncertain
Eccentricity: 0.009
Albedo: 0.6
Visual magnitude: 14.0
Special characteristics: a co-orbital, along with Epimetheus, with which it
   repeatedly exchanges orbits

Epimetheus (J. Fountain, S. Larson, 1966)
Diameter: 120 km/75 mi
Distance from Saturn: 151,000 km/94,000 mi
Orbital period: 16 hours, 41 minutes
Mass: uncertain
Gravity: uncertain
Eccentricity: 0.007
Albedo: 0.5
Visual magnitude: 15.0
Special characteristics: a co-orbital, along with Janus, with which it repeatedly
   exchanges orbits

Mimas (W. Herschel, 1789)

Diameter: 390 km/240 mi

Distance from Saturn: 187,000 km/116,000 mi

Orbital period: 22 hours, 36 minutes

Mass: 0.0005

Gravity: 0.0069

Eccentricity: 0.02

Albedo: 0.8

Visual magnitude: 12.5

Special characteristics: displays one especially large crater that suggests a collision that nearly smashed this moon

Enceladus (W. Herschel, 1789)

Diameter: 500 km/300 mi

Distance from Saturn: 238,000 km/148,000 mi

Orbital period: 1 day, 8 hours, 53 minutes

Mass: 0.0011

Gravity: 0.0089

Eccentricity: 0.004

Albedo: 1.0

Visual magnitude: 11.8

Special characteristics: among the most reflective objects in the Solar System; very white ice-covered surface with few craters

Tethys (G. Cassini, 1684)

Diameter: 1,060 km/650 mi

Distance from Saturn: 295,000 km/183,000 mi

Orbital period: 1 day, 21 hours, 19 minutes

Mass: 0.0103

Gravity: 0.0188

Eccentricity: 0

Albedo: 0.8

Visual magnitude: 10.3

Special characteristics: icy and heavily cratered; the two small moons nearest it orbit in the same path, one 60 degrees ahead and the other 60 degrees behind this moon

Calypso (Pascu, Seidelmann, Baum, Currie, 1980)
Diameter: 25 km/16 mi
Distance from Saturn: 295,000 km/183,000 mi
Orbital period: 1 day, 21 hours, 19 minutes
Mass: uncertain
Gravity: uncertain
Eccentricity: 0
Albedo: 1.0
Visual magnitude: 18.0
Special characteristics: orbits 60 degrees ahead of Tethys in same path

Telesto (Smith, Larson, Reitsema, 1980)
Diameter: 25 km/16 mi
Distance from Saturn: 295,000 km/183,000 mi
Orbital period: 1 day, 21 hours, 19 minutes
Mass: uncertain
Gravity: uncertain
Eccentricity: 0
Albedo: 0.7
Visual magnitude: 18.0
Special characteristics: orbits 60 degrees behind Tethys in same path

Dione (G. Cassini, 1684)
Diameter: 1,120 km/700 mi
Distance from Saturn: 378,000 km/235,000 mi
Orbital period: 2 days, 17 hours, 41 minutes
Mass: 0.0143
Gravity: 0.0233
Eccentricity: 0.002
Albedo: 0.6
Visual magnitude: 10.4
Special characteristics: heavily cratered; Helene orbits 60 degrees ahead of it

Helene, or 1980S6 (P. Laques, J. Lecacheux, 1980)
Diameter: 30 km/19 mi
Distance from Saturn: 378,000 km/235,000 mi

Orbital period: 2 days, 17 hours, 41 minutes
Mass: uncertain
Gravity: uncertain
Eccentricity: 0.005
Albedo: 0.6
Visual magnitude: 18.0
Special characteristics: orbits 60 degrees ahead of Dione in the same path

Rhea (G. Cassini, 1672)
Diameter: 1,530 km/950 mi
Distance from Saturn: 526,000 km/327,000 mi
Orbital period: 4 days, 12 hours, 24 minutes
Mass: 0.0339
Gravity: 0.0296
Eccentricity: 0.001
Albedo: 0.6
Visual magnitude: 9.7
Special characteristics: cratered and icy, with white streaks of fresh ice deposits

Titan (C. Huygens, 1655)
Diameter: 5,150 km/3,200 mi
Distance from Saturn: 1,221,000 km/759,000 mi
Orbital period: 15 days, 22 hours, 41 minutes
Mass: 1.8309
Gravity: 0.1410
Eccentricity: 0.029
Albedo: 0.2
Visual magnitude: 8.4
Special characteristics: one of the largest moons; only moon with an extensive atmosphere, which is mostly nitrogen and has a surface pressure about 1.6 times that of Earth; atmosphere colored orange by a smog of organic material

Hyperion (W. Bond, G. Bond, W. Lassell, 1848)
Diameter: 255 km/160 mi

Distance from Saturn: 1,481,000 km/920,500 mi
Orbital period: 21 days, 6 hours, 37 minutes
Mass: uncertain
Gravity: uncertain
Eccentricity: 0.104
Albedo: 0.3
Visual magnitude: 14.2
Special characteristics: has irregular shape; has probably been broken up in collisions with other moons, asteroids, or meteoroids

Iapetus (G. Cassini, 1671)
Diameter: 1,460 km/910 mi
Distance from Saturn: 3,561,000 km/2,213,000 mi
Orbital period: 79 days, 7 hours, 57 minutes
Mass: 0.0256
Gravity: 0.0245
Eccentricity: 0.028
Albedo: 0.08–0.4
Visual magnitude: 11.0, but variable
Special characteristics: has two sides of vastly different brightness, bright side mostly ice, dark side of unknown material

Phoebe (W. Pickering, 1898)
Diameter: 220 km/137 mi
Distance from Saturn: 12,960,000 km/8,055,000 mi
Orbital period: 550 days, 11 hours, 2 minutes
Mass: uncertain
Gravity: uncertain
Eccentricity: 0.163
Albedo: 0.05
Visual magnitude: 16.5
Special characteristics: revolves in direction opposite to that of other moons of Saturn; unusual orbit probably indicates that it is a captured asteroid; appears to be more rocky than icy, unlike the other Saturnian moons

URANUS (15)
Cordelia, or 1986U7 (*Voyager 2, 1986*)
Diameter: 40 km/25 mi
Distance from Uranus: 49,700 km/30,900 mi
Orbital period: 8 hours
Mass: uncertain
Gravity: uncertain
Eccentricity: uncertain
Albedo: <0.1 (less than 0.1)
Visual magnitude: >22.9 (greater than 22.9)
Special characteristics: may act as a shepherd moon for a ring of Uranus

Ophelia, or 1986U8 (*Voyager 2, 1986*)
Diameter: 50 km/30 mi
Distance from Uranus: 53,800 km/33,400 mi
Orbital period: 9 hours
Mass: uncertain
Gravity: uncertain
Eccentricity: uncertain
Albedo: <0.1
Visual magnitude: >22.6
Special characteristics: may act as a shepherd moon for a ring of Uranus

Bianca, or 1986U9 (*Voyager 2, 1986*)
Diameter: 50 km/30 mi
Distance from Uranus: 59,200 km/36,800 mi
Orbital period: 10 hours, 24 minutes
Mass: uncertain
Gravity: uncertain
Eccentricity: uncertain
Albedo: <0.1
Visual magnitude: >22.6
Special characteristics: none known to be of particular interest

Cressida, or 1986U3 (*Voyager 2, 1986*)
Diameter: 60 km/37 mi

Distance from Uranus: 61,800 km/38,400 mi
Orbital period: 11 hours, 7 minutes
Mass: uncertain
Gravity: uncertain
Eccentricity: uncertain
Albedo: <0.1
Visual magnitude: >22.2
Special characteristics: none known to be of particular interest

Desdemona, or 1986U6 (*Voyager 2,* 1986)
Diameter: 60 km/37 mi
Distance from Uranus: 62,700 km/39,000 mi
Orbital period: 11 hours, 24 minutes
Mass: uncertain
Gravity: uncertain
Eccentricity: uncertain
Albedo: <0.1
Visual magnitude: >22.2
Special characteristics: none known to be of particular interest

Juliet, or 1986U2 (*Voyager 2,* 1986)
Diameter: 80 km/50 mi
Distance from Uranus: 64,600 km/40,150 mi
Orbital period: 11 hours, 48 minutes
Mass: uncertain
Gravity: uncertain
Eccentricity: uncertain
Albedo: <0.1
Visual magnitude: >21.5
Special characteristics: none known to be of particular interest

Portia, or 1986U1 (*Voyager 2,* 1986)
Diameter: 80 km/50 mi
Distance from Uranus: 66,100 km/41,100 mi
Orbital period: 12 hours, 19 minutes
Mass: uncertain

Gravity: uncertain

Eccentricity: uncertain

Albedo: <0.1

Visual magnitude: >21.5

Special characteristics: none known to be of particular interest

Rosalind, or 1986U4 (*Voyager 2,* 1986)

Diameter: 60 km/37 mi

Distance from Uranus: 69,900 km/43,400 mi

Orbital period: 13 hours, 24 minutes

Mass: uncertain

Gravity: uncertain

Eccentricity: uncertain

Albedo: <0.1

Visual magnitude: >22.2

Special characteristics: none known to be of particular interest

Belinda, or 1986U5 (*Voyager 2,* 1986)

Diameter: 60 km/37 mi

Distance from Uranus: 75,300 km/46,800 mi

Orbital period: 14 hours, 54 minutes

Mass: uncertain

Gravity: uncertain

Eccentricity: uncertain

Albedo: <0.1

Visual magnitude: >22.2

Special characteristics: none known to be of particular interest

Puck, or 1985U1 (*Voyager 2,* 1985)

Diameter: 170 km/106 mi

Distance from Uranus: 86,000 km/53,400 mi

Orbital period: 18 hours, 19 minutes

Mass: uncertain

Gravity: uncertain

Eccentricity: uncertain

Albedo: 0.07

Visual magnitude: 20.3

Special characteristics: none known to be of particular interest

Miranda (G. Kuiper, 1948)
Diameter: 485 km/300 mi
Distance from Uranus: 129,900 km/80,700 mi
Orbital period: 1 day, 9 hours, 55 minutes
Mass: 0.001
Gravity: 0.0089
Eccentricity: 0.017
Albedo: 0.34
Visual magnitude: 16.5
Special characteristics: one of the most varied and exciting of surfaces, with
    features including craters, grooves, mountains, and giant cliffs

Ariel (W. Lassell, 1851)
Diameter: 1,160 km/720 mi
Distance from Uranus: 190,900 km/118,600 mi
Orbital period: 2 days, 12 hours, 30 minutes
Mass: 0.018
Gravity: 0.0277
Eccentricity: 0.0028
Albedo: 0.4
Visual magnitude: 14.0
Special characteristics: many large canyons and signs of fluid flow across the
    surface

Umbriel (W. Lassell, 1851)
Diameter: 1,190 km/740 mi
Distance from Uranus: 266,000 km/165,000 mi
Orbital period: 4 days, 3 hours, 30 minutes
Mass: 0.017
Gravity: 0.0249
Eccentricity: 0.0035
Albedo: 0.19
Visual magnitude: 14.9
Special characteristics: darkest of the large Uranian moons; has only one bright
    feature, which seems to be a crater floor

Titania (W. Herschel, 1787)
Diameter: 1,610 km/1,000 mi
Distance from Uranus: 436,000 km/271,000 mi
Orbital period: 8 days, 16 hours, 54 minutes
Mass: 0.047
Gravity: 0.0372
Eccentricity: 0.0024
Albedo: 0.28
Visual magnitude: 13.9
Special characteristics: largest of Uranus's moons; covered with many craters

Oberon (W. Herschel, 1787)
Diameter: 1,550 km/960 mi
Distance from Uranus: 583,400 km/362,500 mi
Orbital period: 13 days, 11 hours, 7 minutes
Mass: 0.0397
Gravity: 0.0338
Eccentricity: 0.0007
Albedo: 0.24
Visual magnitude: 14.1
Special characteristics: rayed craters filled with muddy ice

NEPTUNE (8)
1989N6 (*Voyager 2, 1989*)
Diameter: 50 km/30 mi
Distance from Neptune: 48,200 km/29,900 mi
Orbital period: 7 hours, 10 minutes
Mass: uncertain
Gravity: uncertain
Eccentricity: uncertain
Albedo: uncertain
Visual magnitude: uncertain
Special characteristics: none known to be of particular interest

1989N5 (*Voyager 2,* 1989)
Diameter: 90 km/56 mi
Distance from Neptune: 50,000 km/31,000 mi
Orbital period: 7 hours, 30 minutes
Mass: uncertain
Gravity: uncertain
Eccentricity: uncertain
Albedo: uncertain
Visual magnitude: uncertain
Special characteristics: none known to be of particular interest

1989N3 (*Voyager 2,* 1989)
Diameter: 140 km/87 mi
Distance from Neptune: 52,500 km/32,600 mi
Orbital period: 8 hours
Mass: uncertain
Gravity: uncertain
Eccentricity: uncertain
Albedo: uncertain
Visual magnitude: uncertain
Special characteristics: none known to be of particular interest

1989N4 (*Voyager 2,* 1989)
Diameter: 160 km/100 mi
Distance from Neptune: 62,000 km/38,500 mi
Orbital period: 9 hours, 30 minutes
Mass: uncertain
Gravity: uncertain
Eccentricity: uncertain
Albedo: uncertain
Visual magnitude: uncertain
Special characteristics: none known to be of particular interest

1989N2 (*Voyager 2,* 1989)
Diameter: 200 km/120 mi
Distance from Neptune: 73,600 km/45,700 mi

Orbital period: 13 hours, 18 minutes
Mass: uncertain
Gravity: uncertain
Eccentricity: uncertain
Albedo: uncertain
Visual magnitude: uncertain
Special characteristics: none known to be of particular interest

1989N1 (*Voyager 2,* 1989)
Diameter: 400 km/240 mi
Distance from Neptune: 117,600 km/73,000 mi
Orbital period: 26 hours, 54 minutes
Mass: uncertain
Gravity: uncertain
Eccentricity: uncertain
Albedo: uncertain
Visual magnitude: uncertain
Special characteristics: none known to be of particular interest

Triton (W. Lassell, 1846)
Diameter: 2,720 km/1,690 mi
Distance from Neptune: 354,000 km/220,000 mi
Orbital period: 5 days, 21 hours, 3 minutes
Mass: 0.3
Gravity: uncertain
Eccentricity: <0.0005
Albedo: 0.7
Visual magnitude: 13.6
Special characteristics: revolves around Neptune in a direction opposite to
   that of planet's direction of rotation; has an atmosphere of methane and
   nitrogen

Nereid (G. Kuiper, 1949)
Diameter: 340 km/210 mi
Distance from Neptune: 5,510,660 km/3,422,120 mi
Orbital period: 359 days, 10 hours

Mass: uncertain

Gravity: uncertain

Eccentricity: 0.75

Albedo: uncertain

Visual magnitude: 18.7

Special characteristics: very eccentric orbit: distance from planet changes drastically

PLUTO (1)
Charon (J. Christy, 1978)

Diameter: 1,285 km/800 mi

Distance from Pluto: 19,100 km/12,000 mi

Orbital period: 6 days, 9 hours, 17 minutes

Mass: uncertain

Gravity: uncertain

Eccentricity: 0

Albedo: uncertain

Visual magnitude: 17.0

Special characteristics: is closer in size to its parent planet than is the case for any other planet–moon pair

Information for this checklist is based on data gathered from the *Observer's Handbook 1989* (published by the Royal Astronomical Society of Canada, 136 Dupont Street, Toronto, Ontario M5R 1V2), and from *Sky and Telescope Magazine,* October, 1989 (Sky Publishing Corporation, 49 Bay State Rd., Cambridge, Mass. 02138).

Accretion, 112
Adrastea, 130
Albedo, 20, 123, 128
Amalthea, 64, 130
Amor, 117
Ananke, 65, 134
Andrastea, 65, 130
Apollo Moon Project,
  27, 30, 31, 32–35
Apollo objects
  (asteroids), 117
Ariel, 86, 90, 91, 144
Asteroids, 14, 116–120
  binary, 118
  captured, 46, 64,
    65, 74, 75
Astronauts, 28, 29

Astronomical Unit (AU),
  16
Atlas, 82–83, 105
AU. *See* Astronomical
  Unit

Barringer Meteor
  Crater, 25
Belinda, 94, 143
Bianca, 94, 141
Binary asteroids, 118
Bode, Johann, 116

Callisto, 53–56, 57,
  58, 132
Calypso, 78, 138

Carbonaceous
   chondrites, 46
Carme, 65, 134
Cassini division, 81
Celsius temperature
   scale, 15–16
Ceres, 116, 117
Charon, 110–114, 148
Clarke, Arthur C., 72
Clocks, 24
Comets, 12, 120–126
Constellations, 13
Cordelia, 94, 95, 96,
   141
Core, 26
Craters, 25
   Barringer Meteor
      Crater, 25
   Callisto, 55, 56
   Deimos, 45–47
   Dione, 77
   Ganymede, 56–57
   Mars, 42
   Mimas, 80
   Moon, 25, 26, 27,
      29, 30, 31
   Oberon, 86, 87
   Phobos, 43, 45
   Rhea, 75, 76
   Tethys, 78
   Titania, 88
   Umbriel, 89
Cressida, 94, 141–142
Cruikshank, Dale P., 98

Deimos, 39–50, 75, 129
Desdemona, 94, 142
Dione, 77–79, 138
Duke, Charles M., Jr.,
   29

Earth, 70
   albedo of, 20
   center of universe,
      53
   core, 26
   effect of Moon, 26–
      27
   magnetic field, 51–
      52
Eccentricity, 19, 128
Eclipses, 22–23
   lunar, 23
   Pluto and Charon,
      112–113
   solar, 22
Elara, 65, 133
Enceladus, 20, 78, 137
Encke division, 81
English system, 15
Epimetheus, 80–81, 136
Europa, 55, 58–59, 131
Explorer I, 51

Fahrenheit temperature
   scale, 15–16

Galilean moons
    Callisto, 53–56,
        57, 58, 132
    Europa, 55, 58–59,
        131
    Ganymede, 55, 56–
        58, 132
    Io, 55, 59–63, 131
Galileo Galilei, 13, 25, 53
Galileo spacecraft, 52
Galle, Johann
    Gottfried, 97
Ganymede, 55, 56–58,
    132
Gauss, Carl Friedrich,
    116
Gravity, 19–20, 26, 32,
    49, 97, 118
Gulliver's Travels
    (Swift), 39

Hall, Asaph, 40, 43
Halley's comet, 12,
    120, 122–123
Hector, 118
Helene, 77–78, 138–139
Heliopause, 108
Herschel, William, 86,
    97
Himalia, 64, 133
Hyperion, 71–72, 139

Iapetus, 72–74, 140

Industrial resources,
    36, 50
Io, 55, 59–63, 65, 131

Janus, 80–81, 136
Japan, 123
Juliet, 94, 142
Juno, 117
Jupiter, 51–52, 115,
    116, 117
        moons, 13, 14, 52–
            66, 130–135
        radiation zone, 52,
            53, 64
        rings, 65
        sulfur torus, 62

Kelvin temperature
    scale, 16
Kuiper, Gerard P., 87,
    98

Lagrangian points, 78
Lassell, William, 86,
    98
Leda, 65, 132
Lunar eclipse, 23
Lysithea, 65, 133

Magnetic field, 51, 99,
    107

see also Radiation
  belts
Maria, 30–31
Mariner spacecraft
  missions, 42–43
Mars, 38–42, 115, 116,
  117
    moons, 13, 39–50,
    129
Meteorites, 12, 118–119
Meteoroids, 25, 26, 30,
  31
Meteors, 12, 27
Methane, 98
Metis, 65, 130
Metric system, 15
Micromégas (Voltaire),
  39
Mimas, 80, 137
Miranda, 87, 90, 92–94,
  144
Moon, 15, 24–37, 128
  core, 26
  craters, 25, 26,
    27, 29, 30, 31
  eclipse, 22–23
  effect on the
    earth, 26–27
  exploration of, 27–
    30
  formation of, 25–26
  gravity on, 32
  industrial
    resources, 36
  life on, 37

phases of, 21–22,
  24
religion and, 13,
  24
rocks, 27, 30, 31,
  32
seas, 30–31
space stations, 32,
  36
superstitions
  concerning, 24
worship, 13
Moons, 11–12
  eclipses, 23
  first sightings,
    13–14
  formation of, 26
  motion, 17–20
  reflectivity, 20–21
  see also specific
    planets
MRKOS comet, 124

National Commission on
  Space, 32, 36, 119
Neap tides, 27
Neptune, 97–99, 110,
  112
    moons, 14, 100–108,
    145–148
    rings, 99–102
Nereid, 98, 103, 108,
  147
1989N1, 100, 103, 147

1989N2, 100, 101, 146–147
1989N3, 100, 146
1989N4, 100, 146
1989N5, 101, 102, 146
1989N6, 101, 102, 145

Oberon, 86–87
Oort cloud, 120
Ophelia, 94, 95, 96, 141
Orbit, 17–20
    comets, 120
    Lagrangian points, 78
    retrograde, 98, 107–108
    Pluto, 110
Ores, 36

Pallas, 117, 118
Pandora, 82–83, 136
Pasiphae, 65, 134
Phobos, 39–50, 75, 129
Phobos spacecraft, 49
Phoebe, 74, 140
Piazzi, Giuseppe, 116
Pioneer spacecraft, 81, 108
"Pioneering the Space Frontier" (report), 119

Planetesimal, 112
Planets
    formation of, 26
    moons, 13–14, 26
    see also specific planets
Pluto, 109–110, 115
    moons, 110–114, 148
Portia, 94, 142–143
Prometheus, 82–83, 135
Puck, 94, 143

Radiation belts
    Earth, 51–52
    Jupiter, 52, 53, 64
    Saturn, 67, 71
Radio waves, 62
Reflectivity, 20, 128
Regolith, 30
Religion, 13, 24
Retrograde orbit, 98, 107–108
Revolution, 17–20
Rhea, 23, 75–76, 139
Rings
    Jupiter, 65
    Neptune, 99–102
    Saturn, 79, 81–83
    Uranus, 96
Rocks, Moon, 27, 30, 31, 32
Rosalind, 94, 143
Rotation, 20, 71–72

Satellites, natural.
    See Moons
Saturn,
    moons, 13, 14, 20,
        23, 67–83, 135–
        140
    radiation belt, 67,
        71
    rings, 79, 81–83
Seas, lunar, 30–31
Sinope, 65, 135
Smog, Titan, 68–70
Solar eclipse, 22–23
Solar System,
    formation of, 25,
        26, 55, 93, 112
    general makeup, 11–
        14
Soviet space exploration,
    41, 49, 123
Space stations, 32, 36,
    41
Spring tides, 27
Stars, 13
Stickney crater, 43, 45
Sulfur torus, 62
Sun
    Pluto's distance
        from, 110
    solar eclipse, 22–
        23
Superstitions, 24
Swift, Jonathan, 39
Tago-Sato-Kasaka comet,
    125

Telescopes
    asteroids, 117
    first sightings of
        moons, 14, 20, 39
    function on Moon,
        36
    Galileo's use of,
        13, 25
    Mars' moons, 40
    Neptune's moons, 98
    Pluto's moon, 110,
        111, 112
    Saturn's rings, 81
Telesto, 78, 138
Temperature
    Neptune, 99
    scales, 15–16
Tethys, 78–79, 137
Thebe, 64, 131
Tides
    Earth, 27
    Io, 60
    Phobos, 48
Titan, 68–71, 139
Titania, 87–88
Titius, 116
Tombaugh, Clyde,
    110
Triton, 98, 101, 104–
    108, 147
Trojans, 117
2001: A Space Odyssey
    (Clarke), 72
Umbriel, 86, 89, 144
Uranus, 84–86

moons, 13, 14, 86–96, 141–145
    rings, 96

Van Allen Belts, 51
Van Allen, James, 51
Vesta, 117
Victoria, 118
Viking orbiters, 43–47
Visual magnitude, 128
Volcanoes, 25, 26
    Io, 60, 61, 62, 63, 65
    Triton, 106, 107, 108

Voltaire, 39
Voyager spacecraft
    missions, 14
    Jupiter, 52–53, 59–61, 64, 65
    Neptune, 97–108
    Saturn, 67–68, 72–73, 81, 82, 83
    Uranus, 84–96

War of the Worlds
    (Wells), 41
Wells, H.G., 41

ABOUT
THE
AUTHOR

Joseph W. Kelch is a producer for the Davis Planetarium at the Maryland Science Center in Baltimore, Maryland, where he helps create and present programs for the general public and school groups.

Mr. Kelch was born in Rochester, New York, and graduated from the State University of New York College at Oswego. He had his internship in planetarium operation at the Hayden Planetarium in New York City.